MIRACLE CHILD

Life without the possibility
to see day light

ERROL SCOTT

CONTENTS

CHAPTER 1

WHERE IS MY LIFE

here is my life? What happened to all I had? How did I fall in the trap? Who can I depend on now? When will I ever see freedom again? Never!!! My life started in 1987, born to a crack head mother and a drug dealing father. I was six months old when I had my first taste of crack. My mouth was numb, and I was getting rushed to Martin Luther King Jr. (MLK) hospital to the intensive care unit (ICU). The doctors didn't know if I was going to make it after I swallowed an eight-ball of crack I'd seen on the bed. Now, how are my parents going to explain that? All hell is about to break loose! Who was to blame, my drug dealing father or my crack head mother? Take a good guess! A nanny who didn't exist and somehow no one could ever find her. I was taken by the Child Protective Service (CPS) for the next six months while they investigated the issue. They never came up with what happened, so they gave me back to my parents. They still don't know how I made it alive with only minor complications.

Everyone said I was a miracle baby. I've looked at pictures and lab results, so I know I was supposed to be dead for sure. I had more tubes and wires hooked up to me then a hybrid engine car. Furthermore, I read the newspapers stating my heart stopped 103 times and I stopped breathing 75 times, but they never gave up on me. Not only that, but I have to thank those doctors and the grace of God that I'm alive today. Likewise, I must say, MLK hospital has given life to one who had no life left.

For my first birthday, I had more toys and baby things than a kid could ever imagine, I'm just reminiscing about my baby pictures. I had every kid helping organization in the world giving gifts to me, even all the way out of the country. I had things to last until I was a teenager, and I should have never wanted for anything. Furthermore, I was the kid growing up with a Mercedes-Benz waiting for me to be able to drive. Whatever year I was willing to learn how to drive would be the year I would receive it. My life was made from just being born after six months on this earth.

Every year after my first birthday, the same abundance of gifts came in. The crazy part is, as soon as it came in the front door, it went out the back door faster than it was received. My mother sold everything she could get her hands on just to get her next hit. It was her way of living and her standard of life. She was overjoyed that I made it to my next birthday and Christmas. Christmas was the end of the year and my birthday was the middle of the year in June. She would divide all the gifts up according to the months to come, so she could get high whenever she wanted. As the years went by, I had gotten older, so the gifts became much pricier and worth much more. By the time I was five, I had received over 2 million dollars worth of gifts.

My father walked out on my mother when I turned 3 because she wanted to avoid getting help. He couldn't get custody of me because he had never gone out to get a job to show he was stable. He was too caught up in the drug game to even worry about me or my well-being, in my eyes. Furthermore, he probably wished I would have died that day. Then he could eliminate me from his conscious and have no strings attached to my mother and her crack baby.

My mother told me he got a DNA test on me when I was in the hospital on my deathbed because he wanted nothing to do with me. When he found out I was his, he kissed me on the forehead and said, "I know one day you will wish you had died today." The only reason I knew his exact words was not because I heard them and remembered them myself. It wasn't because my mother or even the doctors who were there that day told me. Nor did my father later on in life tell me what he said; I watched it come out his mouth with my own eyes.

The day before I became legally blind, I saw my father lips say each word on a videotape that was filmed the day he was in the hospital looking over me, nearly dying. I found the tape in a box of Super Nintendo games that I was about to sell to a collector of video games from the late 80s, early 90s. Written on the tape was "The Closest to Death One Has Ever Been". I thought it was just a mere movie that came out, and my parents liked it, so they recorded it on a tape. I almost sold it with the video games because VHS is well out of date, but I just so happen to have a DVD/VHS player, so I put it in.

To my surprise I see me, my mother and my father. It was from the day I was in the hospital, hanging on for dear life. I can see them saying my heart has stopped. Next, my breathing stopped, and they began doing everything in their power to keep me alive. The scariest part about it is they pronounce me dead. Everyone is in a state of shock because for five straight minutes I'm dead. All of a sudden, I started moving, I was back. They yell, "He's alive, He's alive." Then, the tape went blank and when it cut back on, I see the time and date on the clock and calendar to be three weeks later. My father was standing over me and his lips are moving, but you can't hear his voice. So, I rewind the tape and read his lips, he said, "Die now or one day you will wish you had of died today." I look at the calendar to see it was twenty-one years from the day he said that and the exact time and date. May 17th 1988 at 9:17 p.m. and my clock was at 9:17 p.m., but it was May 17th 2009.

I felt my heart skip not one, but several beats, I couldn't believe my eyes. I fainted that very moment and didn't wake up until later that day when the man who wanted the video games knocked on my door. To his surprise, it was open, and he saw me lying on the floor with the remote control to the VCR/DVD player in my hand. He said I was as stiff as a box, so he tapped me a couple of times, then he reached in his pocket to grab his phone and proceeded to call the police.

As he was on the phone providing the details, somehow I woke up. He asked, "Are you okay because you were definitely dead upon my arrival, you were not breathing or moving." I had my eyes open, but I couldn't see. I started panicking yelling and screaming " I can't seeI can't see somebody help call the police call the ambulance my vision is gone." I started knocking things over swinging frantically, beating on my head and rubbing my eyes. I asked him, "Who are you and what have you done to me?" He replied, "I just got here; I'm Larry, the collector, I came to pick up the games. You were stretched out on the floor, remote in hand, with the TV on pause. There's a baby in the hospital with what looks like his father standing over him."

"Yes! Yes! That little boy is me, now I remember I must have dozed off." "No sir, you were not sleeping, you were just as dead as a door knob." "I don't understand Larry, can you please do me a favor and rewind the tape and tell me what that man who is supposed to be my father says to me."? "Ok will do, it looks as if he's saying to try now or Sunday you'll catch fish for dad on Monday." "That made no sense, read it again and make sense of what he's saying." What I saw was, "die now, or one day you will wish you had died today." "Oh my God! Yes, that is what he said, how would you have known that if you're blind?" "Yesterday I could see, well, I had 20/15 vision. I think that seeing my dad say those words to me made me go blind. It also made me pass out to see my father say such hurtful and cruel words like that to me. You know I'm known as the miracle child I'm not supposed to be alive, I swallowed in eight-ball of crack cocaine at six months."

CHAPTER 2

AWAKENING

At the young age of six years old, I started learning jujitsu as a hobby to pass time after I got out of school. My mother didn't have to pay for it of course because I was the miracle child, so everything was free for me. Even at six my mother hardly ever spent any time with me, she was so happy that there were things like karate and Bible study to keep me all day. I only saw her at night, right before bedtime and in the morning right before school.

On the weekends, I was at my grandparent's house or stuck with some random teenager, which was a child of one of her drugged out friends. I never really understood how my mother was able to go days without sleeping, eating, or seeing me. But she made it happen day in and day out, and I was with someone new or at some type of practice. It didn't dawn on me while I was growing up that all this was going on, I guess I was just a product of my environment.

Everything I learned was from some teacher or some teenager that was going through the same or similar things I was going through. The teenagers had no explanation of what was happening or how we were getting treated. I learn so many ways of life, it amazes me to know that there's so much to learn, and you never stop learning.

From the first grade until the 5th grade I didn't even know what my mother's name was honestly, I called her mom, hey you, lady, and mama. Then one day she asked me, "Who loves Mama Rachel" and I looked up and said, "Is that the lady who's coming to watch me tonight." She looked at me as if she saw a monster or a ghost and said, "No that's mommy Jason, Rachel is my name you know that." I said, "Mom, there are a lot of things I know, and your name is not one of them. So, you're the Rachel my teachers and classmates are always talking about. Now I know who they've been referring to all this time. I used to say I was glad that Rachel woman was not my mom; she's a horrible mother, and it must suck being her son. I can't believe that it was you they were speaking on.

So mom, you're on crack? Mom, is what they are saying about you true?" Next thing I know, she broke out into tears. "Did they really say such horrible things to the class on my behalf?" "Yes, mom they say really, awful things about you. Did you really sell all my gifts growing up for drugs, is that true?" "I must tell you everything that they've said is true most likely in some way, shape, or form! I'm sorry, Jason! I'm very, truly sorry, and I want you to believe and know that I'm turning myself into a clinic for help today. You're going to stay with your grandparents for a while until I complete my treatment. I promise I will get cleaned up as of today, March 8, 1994. I will never pick up any more crack, son, I promise! Furthermore, I never realized how I have not been there for you most of your life, son. It's been ten years, and you don't even know my name.

I've failed you since you were a newborn. You almost died on me, and that didn't even stop my crack habits. That's also why your father left me and you alone. He couldn't deal with my addictions anymore. It wasn't because he was a deadbeat dad, as you've probably heard, it was because of me. He tried to get custody of you, but he couldn't. Because the income I had for you from all the people and businesses that donate money and gifts, it was enough to keep him from taking you away from me.

That's why if you remember when you were seven he kidnapped you for a while. I had to do a police report on you as a missing child to get you back." "So that was my dad who had me locked in that room for 107 days until the police raided his house and found me. I never knew that was my dad, mom, I really never knew. I just always thought you had given me away and didn't want me back. He used to give me all the sweets I wanted and let me play the Nintendo all day, but I never went anywhere. Not even to the bathroom, it came to me.

Then one day I heard a knock at the door and a lot of ruckus going on. Some police men opened the door, and then they returned me to you. I never understood why people were always so nice and asking was I ok. The doctor kept asking me had I been touched or tampered with. I just always remember wishing that the man would come back for me. But he never showed up, even though I kept an eye out for him every time the door opened up." "Yes son that was your father, I haven't heard from him since that day the police returned you home.

Now let's get you to your grandparent's house, so I can get myself together. I'm going to pack all of your things up, so you can take them with you and your grandparents will do the rest. They'll be making sure you get to school, karate class, basketball practice, and Bible study. They've been asking me to get clean for years I just couldn't get past my addiction for the love of being high 24/7, 365 days a year.

Your father didn't know I was on drugs for a long time after we started dating, but when he found out, he knew why his stash kept coming up short. I tried drugs for the first time when I was with him. I took it right from his stash because I wanted to see what everybody else wanted so badly. When he found out, he gave me the option of him or the drugs, and I chose the drugs. I didn't think anything was better than chasing that next high. Son, it's un-explainable how it has taken over my life. I've sold so many things that were valuable to me that I should not have sold, it's extremely crazy. I apologize for all that I've done because you didn't deserve any of what I've put you through. Even with knowing you are a blessing from God, I couldn't see the light that should have led me to seeking help.

Now let's get your things packed and ready to go to your grand-parent's house." "Can I take my game and Lucky my pet turtle since I'll be there for a while?" "Sure, and clean your room up while you're at it, it's a little messy." "Mom, are you really going to get clean? Or are you just giving me an excuse to leave me with my grandparents while you go run the streets and get high with all the local crack heads, like everyone says you do?" Pop! My mom slapped the mess out of me right in the mouth. "Don't you ever speak to me that way ever again in life if you want to live to see my age? Forget what other people say. I'm your mother, and you damn sure can believe I would do anything for you.

Today is the day you can put all your trust back into me. Son, I can only show you better than I can tell you. I would rather not hit you like that; you just caught me off guard with your comment. Now stop crying and come here. Everything's going to be alright, I have your back to the end of my time." That was the first time my mother ever slapped me in the mouth, and she used some force from deep within. I made sure I never spoke down or belittled my mother ever again. "Jason I'm really going to get help, believe me I am, because I need your love and trust. As of right now, I feel as if I have neither. If you think and feel that way, I can only imagine how everyone else feels. I never knew that people talked so badly about me and to my son, my only-begotten son at that. It's good to know at least you didn't know that they were talking about me, but they all definitely knew they were mistaken."

CHAPTER 3

GRANDPARENTS

Moving in with my grandparents was not really what I wanted. They were very strict and had more rules than the book "One Million Rules That Can be Broken". Everything was done to perfection, or it was not suitable enough for them. I couldn't drop a crumb without them yelling and screaming at me. When I used the sink in the bathroom, it had its towel to dry it out. I was only able to use 5 sheets of toilet paper to wipe my behind. I was only allowed to wipe 3 times per sitting so that was 15 sheets of a bowel movement. Furthermore, I had to mark down when I took a number 2, so they knew when a new roll of toilet paper was needed. Each roll came with 1000 sheets of toilet paper, so I would get 66 number 2's until another row is needed. Then, there was paper towel and only 2 sheets of that could be used after I washed my hands from my number 2. If you only had to pee, you were to air dry your hands or wipe them on your clothes. There were also Kleenex for blowing your nose, and you could only use them if you had an existing cold. Yes, it gets crazier!! Anytime you use the soap, you were to use one squirt of soap. Oh, and they knew one hundred and ten squirts would come from that bottle. It was the same way for taking a shower. You must take a bath in the tub once a month on the third Wednesday of the month. However, you had to clean the toilet, tub, and sink after every use and if it had stainless steel on it those parts better shine. If you couldn't see your reflection in it, you were mistaken and you'd better fix it. Just from how the bathroom had to be, no one wanted to come visit my grandma and grandpa. When you get to the door you better have your shoes off or untied ready to take them off. If you have on dirty socks, you might as well take them off too because they had clean ones at the door for you to put on. Everyone in the family had a pair of clean socks waiting for them with their names printed. And if you brought company with you, there was a pair for them too. The couches had plastic covers you would put on if you wanted to sit down. Oh, and they hated raggedy cars that leaked oil or other fluids, so rather your car was new or old you parked across the street. You could never park in their driveway or in front of their house. I used to think they hated me as a child because I was very messy; spilling things everywhere and tearing up stuff.

Their house was all white. Everything they owned had a marble top. They both had a white Mercedes-Benz; his and her style, sitting in their four-car garage. My grandfather retired from the military after serving 25 years and 10 deployments. As a Sergeant Major of the Army, he had every school you could go to under his belt. He was Airborne, Air Assault, Pathfinder, Ranger tab, Rangers scroll, Sapper, Sniper, Sears, Combat Diver, and Special Forces. He fought in the Vietnam War, World War 2, Desert Storm, and various little deserts; so you know he has seen a lot of action. My grandmother, on the other hand, retired from the Detroit Police Department. She's been shot twice and stabbed thirteen times from local criminals that have been put behind bars. I heard about her on the news, and kids in my class would call me a snitch because my grandmother was on the police force. I had to fight all the time to prove myself when people would accuse me of being a snitch for no good reason at all.

My grandparents were so strict on me; I don't even know how my mother got into drugs. I had to sneak and eat candy because to them, I was just going to rot my teeth out. Not only that, but I had to brush my teeth three times a day to keep the cavities away, as they would say. Furthermore, I could only play my video games three hours out of the day because there was always something new to learn that they wanted me to know. Likewise, I had a spelling and a vocabulary word definition test every week at their house, even if I didn't have homework. It got to the point where I would fake like I had a lot of homework, so I wouldn't have to do what they were trying to get me to do. They had a plan for every day of the week so that I never stopped learning. Even while I was sleeping, they would play classical music or nature sound, saying, "I could learn while I'm asleep." I used to think it was the craziest idea in the world, but they showed me studies that it was factually true. They have done research on people and learned while sleeping, somehow or another you can learn. I'm not going to lie, I was the smartest kid in my class and grade, but I was just the class clown all day every day.

My grandparents used to go dig up clay out of the ground and eat it every third Sunday. I thought they were just saying it was dirt, so I wouldn't ask for none, until I went with them one day to pick it up. So, you can guess what I did, I went outside and started eating dirt. Not knowing the difference between clay dirt and the regular dirt in front of the house, I would intake mouthfuls. I got sicker than a dog because I ate so much dirt they had to pump my stomach out.

The dirt had clogged up my insides so bad I couldn't eat anything, so they had to feed me through a tube. I was hospitalized for two weeks, I was unable to keep anything down. Everything came right back up as soon as it went down. My grandparents didn't know what was wrong at first, until the doctor told them I was full of dirt. I was the true definition of a dirt bag. Ha Ha Ha!! They really filled up a bag of dirt from my stomach.

They questioned my grandparents for hours about how well they took care of me. Moreover, how often were they feeding me because no one would just eat dirt for no reason? Well, Besides me Ha Ha Ha!! They eventually asked me, "Why did I eat dirt?" I told them straight up, "I thought eating dirt was good for you." I saw them eat it all the time, and they were just fine and dandy. Then they explained to me that they don't eat dirt, it's clay dirt, which isn't all that healthy either. Really, they don't eat a lot of it, just small amounts that their body can handle. Then they said, "I hope you learned a good lesson here. Just because you see someone doing something, doesn't mean you have to follow them." They then asked me, "If we jumped off a bridge, would you follow?" My answer made them worry about my well-being because I said, "If you all jump, it must be safe. Ha ha ha ha!" They didn't know whether I was serious or not because I had the straightest look on my face. I never cracked a smile, and they said, "You have a point there, why would the both of us jump if it wasn't safe at all?"

CHAPTER 4

NO MORE EXCUSES

My mother started crying, saying, "please excuse what I have done to you, and I'm going to try to make up for the lost time." She never intended on being a horrible mother, she just let the drugs oppress her. Even though she missed out on a lot of my life; she was my mother at the end of the day. She could have given me up to an adoption clinic or left me to someone else. The reason she didn't is that she loves me and truly cares about me. I have seen her go through countless struggles to keep me happy. She never gave up on me even when times were rough.

My mom may have been a crack-headed junky, but she carried me for nine months. She kept me in the right place by showing me what was right from wrong and what to do and what not to do. She was my father and my mother because my dad was nowhere to be found at the time.

As we were packing my bags getting ready to go, my mother

saw a picture of my dad. She said, "Here's your father if you want or would like to know what he looks like." I looked and said, "My dad looks like he has a lot of money, is that his Lamborghini Diablo?" "Yes, it is son, and he owns a lot more than just that; he's a multi-millionaire." "Why did he leave you or why did he leave me or why did you leave him?" "It was the drugs, baby!!! The drugs, I couldn't control myself, and they had control of me, and I was unable to let them go. That's why I'm never going back to them; I'm giving them up now because I can't afford to lose the only man left in my life. I've lost so much to this addiction I can't do it any longer, I really can't Jason." "Mom, everything will be okay. I promise everything will be ok, the Lord will help you through it."

"Son, I'm proud of you; I'm actually overjoyed that I had you because you're an angel from above. You've always been strong since you were an infant; you've proven that you can take on anything and get by whatever is in your path. You've never given up, even when you had nothing or any reason to stay strong. Furthermore, you've surprised everyone because you made it alive to have this conversation here right now. Not only that, but you were dead multiple times, but you never gave up. Likewise, you held on for dear life, and that is important in this cold world. If you can do that, then I can stop doing drugs because you're still alive and I am too. I never put it into reality that I have something other people lose every day; a healthy son who is a living miracle that fights every day to get the next breath of air in his lungs." "Mom, I'm not a miracle, I'm just the son of God, only he knows when he wants me to return home." "Yes you are baby, you're absolutely right as long as you're in God's hands you're safe."

"Mom you know I pray for you all the time and definitely at night because I love you. I always pray that one day you are given the chance to recover from what you've been going through. Now

I believe this is God's answer to my prayer's day in and day out. Mom, you really mean the world to me. I always told myself when you would leave me somewhere that you were going to come back a changed woman. Even though I didn't know what was going on, I just would say that to myself. I thought you would come back as the new mother I always dreamed of; one that would not leave her son with strangers who we barely knew.

I have to tell you, a couple of times the girls that you left me with have molested me, but I enjoyed it, that's why I never told anyone. They have put their mouth down there and had sex with me numerous of times, mom, but it was great. I'm in the 5th grade and have already experienced sex, which by the way I like. It's the best feeling in the world, mom; they have really shown me some tricks." "Stop! Stop! Son, what have I done, what kind of mother am I? To let these things happen to you and not even be able to protect you." "Mom, it's okay, I wanted it, I promise I did." "No please, no Lord help me, my son, my only son has been taken advantage of by some little girls. I have to get you to the hospital now and have them check you out. I don't understand how I let this happen; baby I'm sorry, I'm so, so sorry, I swear. How long has this been going on with you not saying anything?" "Mom calm down it's only been a year and a half maybe, but that's all, so it's ok mom." "That's all!!! No, No, No, this can't be happening to me right now, why are you just now saying something." "I told you I liked it, mom. I liked it, so why would I tell you, when I really saw no harm in the enjoyed sexual activities."? "My baby, oh why me and my baby? What have I done, lord, what have I done? How will I ever make up for this? Son, I apologize dearly, I never meant for this to happen." "Mom, what's so bad about it because they told me that's how I got here so what's the big deal." "Baby, the big deal is that you've been molested son; do you hear me, you've been taken advantage of right in front of my eyes? You're not supposed to know what sex is, and definitely not what it feels like. You're a little boy, not a grown man. I'm going to have to live with the fact that your virginity has been taken for the rest of my life. You can never get that back once it's gone, it's gone. Which one of those little skanks did such a thing? Please tell me which one." "I don't know them by name, mom, but I promise I wouldn't tell who did it anyway." "Is that right you promise, huh, that don't mean a damn thing. So now you tell me at last! Who did it?

Now let's go leave everything the way it is; you've got to get to the doctor office to make sure you're OK." "Mom I'm fine, I'm fine I feel great I don't need to go to the doctor they have needles. I don't like needles, mom, please don't take me to the doctor's office." "Son, you have to get checked for STDs and see if you're okay down there. You don't know what they could have given you." "What's an STD, mom?" "Sexual Transmitted Disease see, that's my point exactly; you have no clue about sex and its complications. I thought I still had time before I had to have this talk with you, but clearly not." "How do you get that, do only girls have it first?" "Son it comes from unprotected sex when germs get passed from one person to another which can be deadly or harmful to you. Those girls could have been getting raped as well by someone who has an STD. That can be terrible for you and them because you can pass it without knowing that you have it. Unless you get checked out by a doctor to make sure you don't have anything. Some of them aren't curable; they stay with you your whole life and make you sick. You have no idea, son, what all can come from sexual activities. That's why we have babies having babies all the time, now come on, we have to get you to the hospital right now."

CHAPTER 5

EXPERIENCES

"Mom, can I ride in the front seat today, I'll be still and wear my seatbelt."? "I guess this one time you can, but you must promise to stay in your seat belt." "Okay, I promise mommy I'll be good and stay in my seatbelt." "Come up here, Jason, and I'll buckle you in for the ride." My mom backed out the driveway, headed for the hospital. In about 5 minutes after we were driving, we saw a car accident right in front of us as we were driving. My mom slammed on the brakes and said, "now do you see why it's important to wear your seatbelt. Look at that man, he's on top of his hood, he flew straight through the window. He had no seatbelt on now he might be dead. His car is totaled, and he's probably in critical condition from the looks of the car wreck. Look at that baby in the car seat in the back seat of his car, I hope she's alright, with her long pretty hair and her pink sundress. I should stay here to give the police the information on what led up to the accident. Also see if they're OK or what not so that they can be taken care of and get to the hospital. Stay right here, son, I'm going to go check the condition of the people in the accident."

My mom opened the car door and walked over to the car, I could hear her voice. "Are you okay sir, can you move your head, please blink if you can hear me but can't move? Hey little one how are you, you look a little shaken up from the accident, are you okay?" "Yes I'm OK I don't know what happened, I was asleep and the next thing I knew the car was crashed. My nose is a little sore and I have a slight headache, that's about all." "How old are you, baby girl?" "I'm 10 years old, we were headed to my cousin's house, she's having a birthday party for her 12th birthday." "Oh ok you stay here and sit tight little mama, I'm going to check on your father. Sir, sir, are you alive, can you hear me, can you move? Somebody call the ambulance, he's not moving or breathing. Help, help, help, he needs medical attention fast. Stay with me sir, stay with me, your daughter requires her father, she really does. Someone check the other car to see if the woman's okay, the police are on the way. I don't know if she's alive, she slumped over in her Cadillac CTS."

I saw the whole thing; she was pulling out of the parking lot of Kmart, and he was driving down the street in front of me in the lane over closest to the median. She almost made it, but he was going faster than she thought. The next thing I saw was her car flipped over, and he flew out his window, landing on his hood. Oh! there's the ambulance, the police, the fire department, and the channel 7 news. How did this all come about what's going on today, disaster after disaster I don't know what to do anymore.

The police walked up to my mom and asked a few questions. I couldn't hear what was being said, but I saw my mom pointing and acting out what happened and how it happened. She paused for a bit, then looked at me in the car; she walked to the car, unbuckled me and brought me over to the police. Then the questioning continued, "So who was in the wrong from your perspective?" "No one honestly they both did the right thing, it just was their timing was a little off which caused the collision." "How far away were you at the time of the crash?" "I was less than maybe 20 yards (18.29 meters) away from them, sir." "Is this your handsome little boy, he looks pretty familiar for some odd reason?" "I'm the miracle baby, you know, the one who everyone wants to interview and give gifts to." "Oh my, that's you I know exactly who you are, but right now, son we have to figure out details with the crash. Ma'am what's your information in case we need you later on because you've answered all the questions I have for you. Therefore, you can continue on your day and whatever you have planned."

I watched the fire department go to work on the woman's car because it flipped over, and the door won't open, so they are trying to saw it off. They finally get it off, and the woman's face is covered in blood as they're pulling her out. The doctors immediately start hooking her up to IV's and the other machines trying to keep her alive. Then a big boom went off, and her car went up into flames, if police had arrived 10 minutes later she would have burned to death.

The man who had been thrown out the window was looking around scared not knowing what was going on. He was still shaken up from the crash and a little in a daze. They put him in the ambulance along with the woman and drove away to the hospital along with the little girl.

My mom picked me up, gave me a hug and a kiss on the cheek. She said, "You see how important it is to be buckled up every time you're in any car, son. That's why I like you in the backseat safe and sound because you never know when an accident is going to happen." She put me in my booster chair, buckled me in and followed the ambulance to the hospital. While we were driving to the hospital my favorite song came on the radio which was Tupac's America's Most Wanted.

We pulled up to the hospital and my mom found a spot to park then we headed to my doctor to get me checked out. He said everything looked alright, but the lab results will come back within a week or two at the most. My mom smiled and had the happiest look on her face that I've seen in a long time. She thanked the doctor and said she'll be back to get the results once he gives her a call.

We left and went back home to finish packing my clothes, so I can go to my grandparent's house. We headed there not too long after we got all packed up, and my grandparents were surely glad to see me. My mother explained what was going on and what her plans were, and boy were they pleased. My mom gave us all a kiss and said, "I'll see you all later."

CHAPTER 6

RECOVERY

My grandparents and I had a ball, we watched movies and played video games all during that summer. My mom called to check on me to see if I was ok and how I was doing. She had heard about me getting sick from eating dirt and we laughed about it. She said she did the same thing before so I'm definitely her son a real dirt ball! Then one day she came to see me right before the summer was over to show me how healthy she was. It was astonishing, she gained about 30 pounds (13.61 kilogram) and had coins that she wanted me to keep close to me to let me know she's really getting well.

We discussed so much, she told me my lab results came back and I didn't have anything. I told her I wanted to go to school from my grandparent's house until she got herself all the way together. My school was closer to their house, plus I had some cool friends in their neighborhood. I let my mom know I was very proud of her and that I wouldn't trade her for anything in the world. She told me that she went on a few dates with the police officer from the accident. He showed her a good time every single step of the way. She let me know how much she loved me and really care for me, and that's why she had to get cleaned up. She left me with the most important key in life, which is to never give up on anything because everything is possible through God.

The school year began, I was was finally in middle school 6th grade and it was great, I learn so much along with what my grandparents have me learning on a day-to-day basis. Then one day my teacher asked me about how my mother was doing it made me smile because I was able to tell her, my mother was doing great, plus I showed her my mother's coins. She knew exactly what they were, she said that was great and to ask her to keep up the good work. Then she went on to say, "To tell you the truth, I went through some of the same things. I had a time in my life where I let my addictions get the best of me, but I eventually got myself together. Your mother is a great woman she found it in herself to do what is right, she deserves a round of applause.

How are your grandparents doing now a day, I see they're keeping you ahead of the game with learning new things? I hope you keep up the good work because they always tell me how hard they push you to do the best. I'm hoping to see them at parent teacher conference this year, we always have a lot to elaborate on, plus your grades have been outstanding this year and your behavior has been exceptional. You haven't gotten into any altercations or had any detention time; you're on the honor roll and all." "It's mainly my mom Ms. Smith that I'm pushing so hard in school for because she has really changed. I'm ready to be back under her care and live with her as my active mother.

What made you go seek help when you were going through your hard times in life? How is the process and did you have someone to help you?" "Jason I had plenty of reasons for getting help,

I didn't want my addiction to go on any longer, it was controlling my life and I couldn't keep letting it. I had too much to lose, my career was on the line and my two children as well. Child Protective Services was at my doorstep and breathing down my neck, ready to take my kids away from me. No one in my family wanted to deal with me because I hurt them so many times throughout the years. I had sold my soul to the devil and everybody knew it, I stole and sold everything valuable in my life. I even stole from my family and friends to the point no one would let me come around anything that could be valuable. Furthermore, I didn't know how bad it was because the drugs took over my life and made me think what I was doing was acceptable.

My parents hated me more than anyone else for the fact that I took so many priceless things from them. I wasn't allowed anywhere near them, I had over 25 restraining orders placed against me from just family and friends. I did damage to everyone that I was able to get close to, it didn't matter who it was. Not only that, but I was out of control and I couldn't do anything about it. Likewise, I loved being high, my mind was unable to get off that subject, I would go days without eating or sleeping to get my next hit.

I've put myself in the most dangerous positions a person could put their self in. I would climb on top of people houses to get through the window to get into the house. Furthermore, I would climb light poles; I did just about anything a person could think to do because I needed a fix. Now you see me as an entirely different person than I was back in those days, how I made it through the storm is by the grace of God himself.

So your mom will be alright I tell you everything will get better, she realizes how much she has to lose. Believe me, she doesn't want to lose you, and you're all she has left at this point. It's hard to look yourself in the mirror after so long, knowing you're losing everything. Life is too short to keep wasting it towards meaningless things.

Jason, I want you to remember a couple of things about life as you grow older, never give up on what you believe in and keep God in your life every day in every way. God will guide you to the finish line at all cost, everything is possible through him, it may seem impossible, but it's not. I went through so much in my life to be right here, able to talk to you about life in general. It's hard to have gone through all I did and live with myself knowing all I know. My life has really changed a lot from where it was, and I hope your mother's life changes for the better as well. Seriously, it's a lot to take in when you start to see yourself doing much better living life again without the drugs."

"Ms. Smith, I'm going to take everything you just told me and make use of it, so I can accept my mom for who she is becoming. I know a lot of the negative things people make my mother out to be, but I know she's so much better than those things they say. I'm happy for her, my grandparents are too, they've been waiting for years for her to get help. They never thought it would happen anytime soon, I really think they had just given up on it. They figured all the time and effort they put into trying to help her, nothing ever worked. She ran from all the help that was thrown her way. My grandparents finally talked to me about it once she decided to get off drugs." "Speaking of them, there they go Jason." "Bye-bye, see you Mrs. Smith after spring break."

CHAPTER 7

MY DAD

"Hey grandpa how's your day been going, mine has been a blast, I've learned some new things about my teacher and about life. It's outstanding how you can see a person a certain way because of the point in life you meet them. So, you can really never judge a book by its cover, like you used to always tell me. I'm really learning numerous key things about everyday life experiences that people go through." "Well, Jason, most people concern themselves so much with what someone else is doing and not what they can do to help the situation." "I'm actually getting to see how much people have to deal with on a day-to-day basis. I never knew what my mom was going through, all I knew is what people said about her, and they didn't even genuinely know." "People see all the bad things, so they really overlook the good because it's just so easy to put people down, and it's hard to build people up." "Then what was my mother life like before the drugs and before all the bad things people know her for now?

What led her to her drug addiction to the point where she took it out of control?"

"You see Jason, your mom was a great woman to be honest, she was the best little girl as a child. She always made the honor roll like you, but she was more of the teacher's pet type of student. Every teacher loved her, she was outgoing, happy, joyful, and full of life, everyone wanted to keep her. It was never a problem trying to get a babysitter for her or to get her to go with other people. I don't know what exactly happened to her over time, it was just something that came about a year before you came into this world. I think it started when she first met your dad, and she was out in the streets every night. Not only that, but I saw her changing little by little as time went by; but never seen the drugs taking over her life. She could have come to me or your grandmother, but she didn't think we would accept what she was going through.

We never really talked to her much about drugs, sex, and alcohol, but we definitely wish we did. That's most likely why she went her route once she got of age, and somewhat of peer pressure. Her mind wasn't ready for what the dark world out there had in store for her, so she got sucked into that life like a vacuum got a hold of her. She started experiencing everything all at once, we found out that she was having sex when one day we were washing clothes and there was a condom wrapper in her panties. We asked her about it, and she said she had been having sex for about 6 months at that time, but she was having protected sex.

We spoke with her at that time, but she had known more than we had in mind to tell her. She learned a lot from sex education at her school, we were amazed at what they taught her. She told us very vulgar descriptions of what STDs were and the symptoms of every one of them. Furthermore, she even told us the causes, where they originated, and which ones you can tell whether you have it or not. It made us delighted and sad at the same damn time, but we respected her decisions at what she wanted to do.

The thing she didn't tell us was that she started drinking and experiencing drugs, which she enjoyed doing occasionally. We later found that out when one day she came home high and drunk after she went to a house party her friends threw. When she came into the house she was loud, giggly and couldn't stop laughing at everything. So, we had a little talk with her about what she was doing to herself, and we didn't accept the fact of underage drinking and drugs. So, she stormed out mad and upset, but we were just trying to protect her from all the evil things drugs do to your life. She just didn't understand what we were telling her because she saw her friends doing it. We knew all about the side effect of drugs and how they make people fall into addiction. She didn't feel as if we were keeping it 100 with her because she enjoyed the high and drunk feeling. She later came back to talk to us about the subject when one of her friends became hospitalized due to an overdose on pain medicine. As well, she was scared to death, her best friend was in critical condition with a little possibility of making it through the week. They projected her to die within 3 days after she made it to the hospital, and they pumped her stomach out. She told us that she never wanted to get high again it wasn't fun or funny anymore it got her to do a reality check. She thanked us for trying to help her before, but she said it was just the phase where she was trying to learn things on her own.

Everything had started to pick back up with her, she got on her feet and knew that her life consisted of so much more than all the fun and partying. She came to us with remorse and sympathy about everything that she had been going through. She told us something we weren't really ready to hear, but we listened and listened well to her. We made her very comfortable telling us any and everything.

She had really understood that we are always here for her and that we love her, regardless of what she goes through.

A year or so went by and that's when she met your father, and she was head over heels for him. She gave us her final notice that she was going to be leaving our home and moving in with your father. Not only that, but she spoke with us for about 3 hours about her plans and that she was going to start working. Likewise, she had a great job at the nursing home, and she had 2 patients that she was going to be taken care of. It made us smile from ear to ear, seeing that our little girl was growing up right in front of our eyes. Your father was a nice gentleman with a lot of respect for his elders. We didn't see him as a bad person at all, he was the coolest guy we have ever seen her around. The third time we had ever seen him, he invited us to dinner and his parents were the surprise guest. That blew our minds that he even thought of such a thing to do on his own. His parents were pretty cool people, they were a cute couple, and they had been married for 11 years at the time. Somehow your father really put a good look in our eyes, we saw of a mature young man. Then we found out later that he was a big time kingpin at a very young age." "Wow, my dad was the man"

CHAPTER 8

FAMILY FIRST

"Grandpa, my father was really that big of a drug dealer that he was known as a king pin?" "Yes he was!" "He was really young, so he must have started at about 15, though. He must have had a lot of money coming in on a day-to-day basis. Maybe that's why my mom was so in love with him because he had money. She seems to like to spend a lot of money, and she was always selling all my things." "Jason, she wasn't hungry for money when she left our house, she was financially stable in our eyes. She started needing money after he left her when she got addicted to drugs. Before that, she didn't need anything at all you would have loved her, she was the cool kid. Your mom really enjoyed life when she was younger and on her own. She partied all the time and loved to travel all over the place. In fact, you were conceived in Jamaica, they were visiting a very nice resort. If I'm not mistaken, it was Hendon where they have a part that everyone walked in the nude."

"Grandpa, you know that when I experience sexual acts by

those girls I enjoyed it, but my mom wasn't so happy. I know I was too young, but I also didn't know I was not supposed to let it happen. No one ever told me about anything involving it, I know now because no one was expecting it to be going on." "Yes Jason it's okay now because we know you had no control, so who can we blame, all we can do now is protect you? It should never have happened, but it's okay now, just know you're safe from this point on. You'll get your time to go through all the things a man is supposed to go through one of these days. I'm sure you're going to enjoy every second of life as a grown up, but for now, please enjoy your childhood because it doesn't last forever. Plus, when it's gone, I'm 100 percent sure that you will want to start back over, but you can't. I know I wish I could turn back the hands of time and do countless things differently than the way they were. I would do a lot more traveling to other countries and exploring the world to get all I can out of it. There are so many things that I didn't get to do that I could have done, but I can say I have no regrets.

You know I joined the military because they drafted me, I really didn't have much of a choice. I enjoyed all the service time I served and all the deployments I went on. Although, fighting was terrifying and hard to deal with seeing your best friends die and get injured. Most of us stayed drunk a lot of the time that we were deployed because it was really hard to stay strong without drinking. If they didn't drink, then they probably used many drugs to stay high the whole time. I've had to carry so many of my friends off the battlefield, dead or alive, it's really a feeling I can't describe. You just have to go through the experience to understand what I saw day in and day out. It made me a lot stronger than I would have ever been if I didn't experience all that I did. There were nights where I couldn't sleep because of all the anxiety I acquired along the way. Some days I can say I felt hopeless to the point that I was unable to get anything productive done. I would just stare off into space, trying to pull myself together from all that was going on around me. Things appear to get worse and worse, at one point I felt like I was chasing death, not my dreams. I knew that it took people like me to keep our loved ones at home safe at night in America. Many people were proud of me for what I was doing, but they didn't understand at the time what I was going through on a day-to-day basis. I knew my job held a certain standard of life for me to live up to, but I didn't know how I was going to make it.

Just to mention the pressure I was under became so stressful; life wasn't the same, my reality was distorted. I was doing things that many others wouldn't and couldn't do, like picking up arms and legs that were blown off. Furthermore, putting clothing around limbs to try to stop or slow down bleeding. I heard people scream-ing at the top of their lungs asking and praying for help, and it hurt my soul. It was horrible watching people take their last breath and begging for mercy. It really hurt when I was trying to save someone, and they died in my arms or if I wanted to save someone, but they would say let them just die. Emotionally, I was torn apart looking for closure, but no one or anything could give me the assistance I needed. There were a few times that I thought killing myself would be a lot easier than dealing with all that was happening around me. Many people did actually commit suicide while we were deployed and once we returned home. I saw what it had done to families time after time. So, I knew I couldn't do it to mine, not after all they looked up to me for. I can say everyone was very supportive throughout the whole time I was feeling depressed.

Your grandmother really kept me headstrong and let me know how much she loves me. Moreover, that she cares so much about my well-being, and she couldn't afford to lose me. It was because of her that I was able to stay sane and not lose my mind. Even though she couldn't quite see what was going on, she watched the news a lot to at least be up-to-date. So, she did see the body count of soldiers being lost and medically disabled. I will never forget the day I called home, and she thought I was dead.

She had seen my name in the papers as one of the deaths that had occurred, but it wasn't me. It just so happened to be another soldier who had the same name as me; she was crying her heart out. She didn't believe it was me she was talking to; she thought someone was trying to cover up my death. It was a lot of that going on to keep people from taking the truth so hard; it was easier to lie at first. Not to mention I had a bit of a cold when I called her, she kept saying I know he's dead, you don't have to lie. Then I told her to ask some personal questions no one else would know, and that's how I got her to see that it was really me. That's when I knew I wasn't fighting any more it was time to come home."

"That's a great story grandpa, may I excuse myself I have to use the bathroom." Once he said sure, I was relieved. Boy, don't grandparents have some stories to tell for days. I went to use the bathroom, then I went to play some video games.

CHAPTER 9

SCHOOL

Before I knew it, spring break was over and back to school I went. I was still getting good grades and speaking with my mom all the time. Parent teacher conference came up and everyone was expecting my grandparents to come. I had a surprise though, my mom came, they were all shocked because she was healthy and a new woman. The last they had seen of her was when she was all cracked out, now she was dressed to impress with 6-inch heels. Grown woman was written on her forehead and her eyes lit up as she strolled in the room. Everyone was congratulating her for the changes she made, plus her and my teacher talked for hours on top of hours. I was happy to see all my teachers proud of my mom, and she was smiling ear to ear; I've never seen her that happy before in my life. After that day, my teachers really respected my mom and I enjoyed coming to school because they always asked how she was doing.

I went through the rest of my elementary and middle school with a breeze. I went to 8th grade prom, and I was the best-looking one there. I took a horse and carriage, all white everything. Furthermore, I had some clean Gator boots that cost $2,000, my suit was tailor-made by Louis Vuitton it cost $5,000, my glasses were Cartier with ice in them, they were $10,000, and all my jewelry came from Jacob the jeweler. So, you know I was fresh to death; no one could compete, plus I had 2 females on my side. Their dresses were Louis Vuitton which cost $4,000 a piece because they were made just for them, their heels were $1,000 red bottoms, and their accessories were Cartier as well. When we arrived everyone was astonished, the looks on their faces were priceless; it seemed as if they saw a ghost. I felt spectacular, and we partied all night long.

I was prom king and both of my dates won prom queen. It was crazy because they both thought the other one was going to win. So, they ended up giving it to both of them because of how we all came together, it made a statement. I also got best dress, baby face, most popular, and teacher's pet in the yearbook; I was just the man all the way around. Plus, I was back living with my mom my whole eighth grade year and still receiving the best gift that a kid could ever want.

That summer was great, I was getting ready for high school and I intended to play basketball. So, I got with the coach that summer because he had been watching me at middle school; I was the best player on the team in my mind. I averaged 23 points, 8 assist, 7 rebounds, and 3 blocks my 8th grade year.

I couldn't wait to see what all the hype was about in high school. I knew the girls were going to be older and more mature. Plus, the environment was going to be intense as far as the games and the rival's games that come to play at our school. I was hoping I wouldn't get into the freshman, fresh meat ordeal. It turned out I knew a lot of the seniors, so I was very popular right off the back.

School was fun; I started off as the class clown, getting put out of class. My teachers didn't understand how my grades were so good, but I couldn't keep the jokes out of the classroom. I had earned a spot on the varsity basketball team, so I really thought I was the man.

I started talking to this girl who was a senior name Malieah, she was beautiful. She had long hair to the center of her back, her breasts were a 34 C, her waist was a 26 and her hips were a 44. Her eyes were hazel green, and Asian like, with the perfect shape nose and lips. She looked like Cassie and had a model walk that made you look twice when you saw her. I had all the students at the school surprised that I got her to date me.

I felt like the man everyday all day; I never had to worry about anything at school. Not only that, but I got into gambling very tough; I would skip class to shoot dice in the hallways in the back of the school. Furthermore, I lost crazy amounts of money shooting dice, plus, I got into a few fights because someone brought trick dice. Likewise, I kept the best gear that came out; I always had a new pair of Jordan's every other week. Furthermore, I was driving an S 550; people didn't know it was mine until they saw my name on the title. Likewise, I went to school just because everyone wanted to see me graduate; life really was already made for me. Not only that, but I partied every weekend and I started renting out buildings to throw parties.

After the 9th grade, I was starting basketball varsity team as the point guard all the way until I graduated. My senior year was crazy because we played a prank on our principal by putting his car on the roof of the school, with tarantulas everywhere. For spirit week, the first day was pajama day, I had a one piece Power Rangers suit on. The second day was 70s day, I had the craziest Austin Powers hippie outfit I could find. The third day was twin day and me and my man's came stupid with the same everything, a $350 Gucci bucket hat, $1,500 Gucci boots, $1,000 Red Monkey jeans, $600 Red Monkey shirt, and $100 Red Monkey draws and socks that were $100 a pair. The 4th day was school colors, so you know I had to go all out. Our school colors were red, white, and blue, so I was American flag down. The 5th day was who can dress the best, so I killed the parking lot with Louis Vuitton everything; it was so crazy, people thought I was their model. No one could tell me anything; I was officially the man of the year.

CHAPTER 10

CHAMPIONS

The senior picnic was at Belle Isle, and boy did we shut it down. Everybody and their momma came out to the park; it was the most anticipated day our school had ever talked about. We had the whole school shut down because freshmen, sophomores, and juniors came to the picnic as well. It was so wild; we made other schools close down their picnic because they wanted to be a part of our history. Besides the teachers and staff, we had people that graduated 4 and 5 years before us come to our picnic. It was crazy how many people showed up that day for the 50th anniversary of our school picnics. There were people you haven't seen in a while that fell off hard and were bums, or people that were major corny and were now getting it popping. The day went well overall; everybody had a great time and really enjoyed their selves.

We were celebrating that our varsity basketball team won state; at which I put up 65 points, 10 rebounds, 12 assists, 11 steals, and 10 blocks. I set and broke records of all time in high school basketball history with a quintuple double. Everybody was going crazy, they have never seen such a show, plus it went into triple overtime. I hit the game-winning basket off a block that I made from off the backboard. I took the ball to half court with two seconds on the shot clock. Furthermore, I shot over two defenders with the ball still in the air as the buzzer sounds. The ball bounced off the rim, hit the clock, then dropped in the basket; the whole building felt like it moved. We had won by one point; the final score was 134 to 135. Everybody ran to the gym floor, I was lifted in the air and carried around the gym and to the locker room. The newscasters and reporters talked to me for an hour after they gave us our trophy.

My girlfriend Malieah stood next to me and whispered in my ear; "You know I'm a put this pussy all over you tonight, and I'm going to bring what you always asked for, another girl in the bedroom. I want you to tear this pussy up like it's your very first time. No making love tonight, fuck both of our brains out, baby. I want you to fuck me from the back while I scream your name. My pussy is already warm, wet, juicy, soft, and feigning your dick baby, I want you right now. I can't wait to put your dick down my throat and swallow every bit of what you have to give me. I wish you were in me right now while my pussy steaming, so I can say harder, harder, right there, I'm about to ejaculate all over you. I'm having orgasms back to back, saying oh daddy I love you don't stop, keep going, to make me cum again. Here it comes now, Daddy; you're the best dick I've ever had. I never want to lose you, Daddy; you know how to hit the right spot. You got my pussy jumping and I can't stop shaking. Oh! I love you daddy, this is your pussy; I promise it's yours baby. Fuck me harder and give me all you got, go in and out of me until I can't move. I feel you coming daddy, let your babies off inside of me. I love your dick, let me taste it for a moment. Then you can continue to fuck the shit out of me and taste this juicy, wet, warm, flavorful, the greatest pussy you'll ever find, after I make your knees shake until you're weak why you say I love it when you ride my dick. Then, when we're done, we can cuddle and caress each other in the soaking wet bed from our sweat, pussy juice, and cum all over the both of us. Next, we can fall asleep from being exhausted and tired. Later we can wake up and start at stage 1 all over again; baby, I can't wait until tonight." I lost track of all the questions everyone around me was asking, I completely zoned out while listening to her.

Then it hit me we won!! We won!! We won this is the greatest feeling in the world and we are the champions. We did it after being down by 15 at the end of the 3rd quarter. Not to mention, our football team also won state the same year, which was crazy as well.

We partied super hard that year, I tell you it was very crazy; so many parties were being thrown. It felt like every Friday someone was having a slamming ass party which led to the biggest party of our senior year, prom and the after party. I was definitely known as the life of the party, so I kept some type of party going.

Prom day oh it was on, you couldn't tell me anything. I had to go ten times harder than my 8th grade prom. Plus, I went pretty hard for Malieah's prom, but now it's my prom, what do you think I did? I went all the way out for this one, I got a Rolls-Royce with the top cut-off, all candy apple red that looked super wet, with cocaine white insides, and it came with doves that flew once I stepped out the car. My suit was tailor-made once again, but this time by Armani. My suit was all red with a white tie and long sleeves. I wore a white Rolex with red Gator boots with white laces and a red top hat, not to mention a white cane. Malieah was clean as fuck too with her red heels and red dress by Fendi; her accessories were made by Cartier. The way they pinned her hair up was the best hairstyle I have ever seen. We took more pictures than a photographer would have taken in a year. We had so much fun dancing and getting drunk as a skunk with all our friends.

After the prom was the biggest and craziest after party I've ever been to. We rented out the whole 21st floor of the MGM casino, and we had a live DJ come through, which was DJ Khaled. Everybody was drunk going in like it was no tomorrow; it was a great night, we had too much fun. The next morning everybody was hung-over and didn't want to move a muscle, totally drained not an ounce of energy.

I was drunk before the night even began because I decided to sneak some Hennessy to the prom. I lost my mind that night at the hotel party that got really crazy; there were people having sex everywhere. So, you know I got it in. I brought a 12 pack of condoms and I used them all on 6 chicks, but I'm not bragging. If you know what I mean, every girl in the world seemed to like me.

After that, we started getting ready for graduation, which we knew some of our class was not going to make it. Yeah, everybody was excited about the fact that we all made it to graduation because it had definitely been a long year for us. So many things happened for us; it was a fantastic year for our sports teams and the parties we threw. Now our day had come to walk across that stage, once our name had been called our high school days would finally be over. As soon as I heard my name, I stood up and said, "Goodbye high school, Hello College."

CHAPTER 11

NBA

The summer after I graduated, I was still trying to decide which college I wanted to attend. I had a full ride scholarship to eight different colleges from the west to the east coast and north to the south. I knew wherever I went it had to be hot year round; I was tired of the snow. My mom wanted me to go to California, Florida, Las Vegas, Texas, or Georgia, so she could visit somewhere nice. My grandparents were very proud of me and all of my accomplishments because they pushed so hard for me to make it.

I went to a couple of summer camps in 2004 when my hometown Detroit Pistons won the championship; I came home for the celebration. It was the craziest after party and celebration. I tell you it was people everywhere and the party didn't stop for about 5 days straight. It was the first time we won a championship since the original bad boys of 1988 when they had Joe Dumars, Isiah Thomas, Rick Mahorn, John Salley,, and Bill Lambier as the starting 5. Now in 2004 we have the bad boys 2 which consisted of Ben

Wallace, Rasheed Wallace, Richard Hamilton, Tayshaun Prince, and Chauncey Billups. I wanted to be a bad boy one day playing for my city because I love Detroit and I would die for my city. So, after the parade I had to get back to business and on my game if I wanted to be a bad boy someday.

I decided to go to Texas A&M after all because I like the weather, environment, women, lifestyle, party life, and southern hospitality. Malieah and I were still together, thinking about getting married not too long after I started college. Not to sound cocky, but I started varsity basketball as the point guard because I was a lot better than the junior that had the position before me.

I also wanted to pledge Sigma because ever since I was young, I always saw them as an inspiration to make it to college. I didn't know all the stipulations of what it took to become a Q-dog, but I was down for whatever. I couldn't mention it to anyone, not even Malieah, but of course, I was unable to keep it from her. She began questioning our relationship because all the time I was spending away from her; so I had to tell her.

She moved in with me after she graduated from Michigan State University with her bachelor's degree in child development. Furthermore, she planned on opening a daycare of her own someday and running it by herself, thanks to some of her family.

I was going to school for business management, but I really had my mind made up on the NBA. I was sure I was going to make it and make my family proud of me. My skills were official, I was the best in the business, there wasn't anyone with a quicker first step than me. Allen Iverson himself told me that after I beat him 21 to 11 in a 1-on-1 match up that I challenged him to. When I won that challenge, I felt unstoppable; I was officially the man to look for when I came out on the floor. Our 1-on-1 was televised on live TV on ESPN, no one thought I was going to win, but in my head I knew if I win my status was going to skyrocket. No one could ever tell me anything after that match up, even if I had lost. People knew I was the truth, even to have the balls to get AI to come play me on national TV.

I really love the game so much, it was nothing anyone could tell me about the game. I studied the greatest players whoever played the game from Wilt Chamberlain, Larry Bird, Bob McAdoo, Magic Johnson, Bill Russell, Shaquille O'Neal, Kobe Bryant, Reggie Miller, and Michael Jordan himself. There's many more, but I can't explain how they played the game and changed the game when they came out on the court. I watched tape after tape of their performances, and it's a really amazing sight to see. To love the game, you have to really appreciate what the legends of the game did. I saw so many last second shots to win the game along with total blowouts those guys have performed. I know some people may think that it is easy to put on a performance as they did, but it's not, it takes hard work. I'm going to put in as much work and time I need, as they did, if I ever intend to be in their shoes. So, I practiced when the scrimmage was over, and after we had a game, I mean all the time nonstop. It has always been fun to me to be able to be all the way turned up. Being able to play basketball and get paid for it is my life, my dream, and my reality.

Nike offered me a contract to wear their shoes for 3.3 million dollars right off the bat. That's when I knew life is about to change for my family name. My mom was getting moved out of the hood and my grandparents as well. I paid my grandparent's house off, and I brought them a house off the Strip in Las Vegas. My mom wanted to go to live off Miami Beach, so I brought her a ridiculously big house off the water. I paid off our little house in Detroit, but kept it just so when I go back, I have somewhere to stay. I let one of my boys rent it out while it set there so no one would break in. Not only that, but I only asked him to give me $50 a month, which was nothing but some chump change to him. Furthermore, I decided that I was going to live wherever my career takes me. Likewise, I wanted a house off the beach as well, so I purchased the home next door to my mother.

I had all types of endorsements coming my way, it was crazy, I went from regular to being an all star still as a freshman in college. Furthermore, I was overwhelmed; I didn't know what to do at that point, my life had become bigger than me. Not only that, but I was wealthy growing up from my earlier accident that almost took my life, now 18 years later I'm on the cover of Sports Illustrated as the man of the year. Likewise, I couldn't go anywhere without paparazzi following me trying to get a story. Furthermore, I felt like the world revolved around me, I was scheduled for multiple interviews back to back. Oprah Winfrey herself wanted to come to my house to interview me and later bring me to her show. Jay-Z & P Diddy was trying to get me in a video shoot for their song. Every commercial wanted me as a cameo for publicity. I was the best thing they had ever seen, I was greater than LeBron, coming straight from high school. No one could stop me, I was at the top of my game.

CHAPTER 12

LIFE CHANGES

Life is a lot different from just 5 years ago, when I was feeling unstoppable and on top of my game my freshman year in high school. I bagged the hottest chick in my school, and she was a senior dating some freshmen. The first day I saw Malieah I was blown away, I just knew she had a man, and I was sure he was at least 21 to 25 or older. Her swag was grown woman and on her shit. She was just still in high school, and she wasn't childish at all. It made me grow up quick, because if I was going to even think about approaching her, I had to come correct. I saw her standing at her locker with a couple of her girlfriends, which were all very popular at our school. So, I had to dig down deep and grab my balls because I couldn't go another second just standing back staring at her.

I was thinking how bad she would really embarrass my freshman ass for having the thought of stepping up to her. I think it came from me watching so many high school movies like 187, Cooley High, How High, American Pie, Light It Up, and You Got Served. Which all had me thinking that it was the wrong answer to approach a senior as a freshman. So, I put a little thought into it and I told myself is she try to play me, I'll act like it was a joke. Hopefully, her boyfriend is not a jock that will be forced to beat me up just because I'm playing around with his girl, you know how that goes. I loosened the straps to my book bag, so that one of my straps hung off, swagged my pants very hard, and walked over to her.

I said, "Hey beautiful, I know you're probably already taken, but I wanted to compliment you on how gorgeous you are. Your man is surely enough blessed to have someone of your class." "Thank you." "My name is Jason, but I go by JR Cash. I'm new to this school, but I've been around a while. You may have heard of me, I'm on the varsity team, I just came from the state winning middle school Brooks. I fell in love with the sight of you standing here; I couldn't let another second go by without manning up and coming to speak to you. I know you probably get people trying to holler at you 24 /7, but I'm a realist and I come to speak my mind, if you know what I mean. Moreover, hello to you ladies as well, not trying to be rude and interrupt your conversation, I saw all of you over here laughing. So, it must have been interesting, whatever you all were talking about. May I have your name, beautiful, so I can further know you and what you're about?"

"My name sweetheart is Malieah and you got some balls to come over to a group of seniors, let alone the most popular ones in the school." She was smiling ear to ear, "Who sent you? One of those crazy ass boys on the team, so you can get cursed out. They set you up for the kill, huh"! She giggled. "Not at all my baby, no one sent me I did this all by myself I thought it through, but I couldn't help but to come over and introduce myself. You looked like a bag of money!" "Aww listen to you, he's really smooth with his words and lips now ain't he all, he is too cool for school."

"I think he deserves a kiss Malieah, he's a cute guy, and he got swag unlike these other bums that be trying to holler at us. He got a little class, and he's only a freshman at that. Check him out with his true religion swag from head to toe, his hazel green eyes, light skin complexion, looking like Trey Songz little brother. He even has the nerve to be standing 6'2" and he balls so hard on the varsity team." "Okay, he gets brownie points for how he carries himself and plus girl you ain't booed up right now, he thinks he's ready." "Okay Monique, he got it coming, come here Mr. Jason or do you prefer Cash, or can I call you my boo thang."? She giggled. "Can I have a kiss from them smooth lips of yours?" All smiles coming for me, I can't stop blushing, I'm feeling like a cornball, but I have to control myself. "Yes you can have a kiss I know you didn't think I was going to turn you down, now did you?" Her lips did not only look soft, but got damn they were very soft as cotton, I wanted to fall into her mouth that very moment. "So Jason, when you're going to take my girl out on a date or something." "I mean damn, bitch you're just giving me away huh, thank you, let us decide what we about to do and when we will do it. Oh! Shit that's the bell, meet me back right here after my class let's out Cash." "Ok, I'll be here after class."

I couldn't stop thinking about her the whole time. My teacher was talking to us about numbers but, I was thinking I have to get Malieah number. Math is my favorite subject, but today math means nothing besides 143 which is love for my new boo. I know she's probably thinking, "He is crazy for coming up to me like he thought he had a chance." I can't believe I actually walked up to her, and she was cool about the situation, I thought for sure she was going to try to play me. Furthermore, I must have really felt some type of way that day to go out my way to even step to her. She was cool as fuck though, she kept it 100 with me, though. I'm going to ask her to let me take her home because I know she may have never been in a s550. If she has, it wasn't mine I don't know if I should play the Pretty Ricky – Blue Star or some big Luther Van Dross, I know she'll like some soft music. What am I going to talk to her about, what should I ask her first, where should our first date be, what turns her on, or what are her pet peeves? So many thoughts were going through my head, I start having a slight anxiety attack. I can't focus at all, she got me all the way gone. She gave me a kiss out the blue, oh boy!! I can't even begin to imagine what she's like in the bed. Now I'm in a daydream…. She's undressing in front of me, she has on hot pink lingerie her ass is fatter than Buffy the Body. Her breast sit up prettier than you can imagine, she's coming closer to me, and she has a whip in her hand with some handcuffs as well I can't control my dick from getting hard.

"Jason, Jason, Jason" a tap on my shoulder from our school security guard. "Are you paying attention and are you ok, you look lost in space? Do you need some water ?" I snapped out of it and looked down; I was hard as a rock. " Oh my you must be thinking about something exciting. You want to pay a little attention there are 10 minutes left in class I wouldn't want you to miss anything important I know this is your favorite class, and you're way ahead of the game. Better yet you're excused you can go, I'll see you to-morrow Jason."

CHAPTER 13

MESMERIZED

That was crazy I was gone with the wind, I totally zoned out thinking about Malieah; she is the most gorgeous woman I've ever spoken to in person, let alone kissed. I was head over heels; I walked to the water fountain and started drinking so much water, I thought the fish was going to die. The minute's seemed to move faster than I thought, and then there goes the bell, time to make a move or be in checkmate. As I saw her coming down the hallway, the hallway went in slow motion. I could see every move her body made. Her hair swayed back and forth as slow as possible, her hips rocked like a boat in stormy weather, her breast bounced up and down as smooth as the bay watch chicks.

My whole world was about to change in 1 moment as we met at her locker. She said, "Hello there, my baby!" It caught me off guard, she used one of my sayings. "Oh, so you must have liked that phrase, I'm guessing!" "Yes, it was pretty smooth; I actually was thinking about you the whole time in class, Mr. Cash." "Oh, is that right, that's what's up, I must have made a good impression on you for the first time coming in contact with you." "Yes, I can say you did, to be honest, most dudes be real lame and corny when they come up to me, or they have someone else come up to me." "Oh yeah, I have another question for you, by the way, can I take you home if you don't mind?" "What we riding the bus together, that's cute, check him out y'all!" I giggled. "Nah, I have a car." "A car, a freshman with the car, oh boy, somebody spoiled. She giggled, "Nah, I just got a long story behind me, you'll soon find out after we chill." "Oh okay what are you driving, I hope not anything worse than riding the bus. She giggled, "Nah, I Drive a s550." "A what, S 550 oh I can't fuck with you honey I knew it was something with you; you're a dope boy, huh? I can't deal with that mess, that's not my type of guy." "Oh! Nah, I don't sell drugs, I don't even like drugs on some real shit I hate drugs they almost cost me my life. I told you I'll tell you more about me in a different setting, can I take you home or not, my baby?" In my mind before she said anything else she went from if my car is busted she can't ride, to my car too expensive, so she can't even fuck with me. Then her voice came rolling off her lips. "Yes, you can take me home you ain't no stalker now, are you?" I giggled, "Nah I ain't on no shit like that Low key I feel insulted, I laughed, you crazy girl." "Nah, nah now days you have to ask because these dudes out here be tripping, wanting to come by unannounced, no call, no text, no message, & I ain't for all that type of shit you feel me." "Yeah, I get where you're coming from all the way." "Let's get on our way, everyone is leaving us." "Okay, I'll see y'all later, ladies." "Bye babes!" "Y'all be safe don't kill our friend, by the way, we're coming to see this car of yours anyway."

"Hey Malieah you can't speak, I guess? Who's your little cousin, that's nice of you showing him around the school?" "No Sam why you are trying to be funny, no I'm not showing him around actually, and he's not my cousin either!" "So what you're doing with that fresh meat that's not you at all, do yo man know about him." He giggled. "First off I don't have a man and second off why you're all in what I'm doing, do your bitch know you're all up in my face, that's the real question! Because I know the bitch doesn't like me or my crew. We stay shitting on her and her lame ass bitches." "Oh, look at Malieah trying to stunt in front of the little fresh meat, check her out." "Aye bruh, you need to calm down with all the fresh meat comments; I'm not even for all that fuck shit you on bruh, bruh." "There go your bitch gone head and run before she comes to pull that ear of yours. You know what it is, that bitch already looking over here." "Aye bruh who the hell are you talking to with yo young ass, don't think because you're with them, you can't get dealt with fool." "Keep it moving Sam, why are you trying to cause a scene and shit, let's go cash!" I mean mugged the shit out of him as I walked away.

"Man I tell you we don't play that fuck shit where I'm from Malieah, he's trying to stunt he's going to get his self hurt. He's thinking because I'm a freshman and a pretty boy, that I'm soft, but he really doesn't want these problems. "Cash don't pay him any attention, he ain't nobody, he just thought you was a little soft or quiet from your demeanor." Once we got outside, I asked her to wait by the front curb I'll bring the car to her, she smiled ear to ear. I heard her friends say, "now that's a real gentleman if I knew one, his parents must be rich and well-mannered." But I'm thinking to myself they don't know the half I'm a let them believe whatever they want to. They will find out soon enough.

I get into the car and change my iPod to Blue Stars, let the sunroof back and pulled up front from out the teacher's parking lot. It felt like everything stopped but my car, I mean everyone at the school mouth hit the floor they couldn't believe their eyes. Yes, it was me and my all black s550 with all white interior and 24 inch

Ashanti's that stood still, no spinning at all. I got out and opened her door and her girls started screaming, "Oh my gosh, can you take us home too please?" "If you don't mind, could you please take them home as well?" She said with a puppy dog face while blushing from ear to ear. "Yeah I got y'all hop in it ain't shit, y'all don't stay across the world do y'all?" "Nah, we stay in the same neighborhood as Malieah." "Oh okay enough said, let's go then, oh and look at what's his name." "Who, Sam?" "Yeah, his damn neck looks broke as his pockets walking over there to the bus stop." They giggled. "I bet he's feeling idiotic now, and I ain't even trying to stunt you feel me that shit petty. Well, y'all are going to have to tell me where y'all stay at unless you type it in the navigation." "How do you work this thing, is it the same way as the GPS people have?" "Yes, just type in your address, and we will be on our way." "Okay, and you thought you were slick turning on some Pretty Ricky." "I mean what you want me to put on some Lil Boosie or some Three 6 mafia because I got some of that on standby, you feel me." "Nah, nah we straight she's just talking don't pay her any attention.

So since you don't sell drugs, what do you do, kill people because don't know regular ninth grade kid from the hood have no s550. And if you're rich, what are you doing going to a school in the hood or is it because they wanted you to play ball with us?"

CHAPTER 14

THE RIDE

"Here's the story simple as I can put it, well, when I was six months old I got a hold of some crack, an eight-ball to be exact I died 103 times. No bullshit at all, so I got everybody in the world involved, I'm pretty sure y'all parents know about me. When y'all go in the house, ask your mom or dad about the Miracle Child back in 1988 they will remember me because it was everywhere in the news. They may have even donated something to me at one time or another. Ever since then, I've been under the care of the world. I have more God parents then everybody you know or heard of. They have been giving me over a million dollars a year, gifts, and money but when I was younger, my mom was a heavy crack head, so she went through most of it if not all of it. I'm still caked up though because I'm still getting money, now my mom straight though she cleaned herself up. It took a while, but she pulled through, so now I'm just enjoying life living with my mom. Malieah you will meet her one day, hopefully if you fuck with me on that level."

"Oh shit, this our block!" "Damn that shit came up quick." I looked around and said, "I got a home boy who stays not too far from here." "Oh yeah, does he resemble you, cash? Came from the back seat. Malieah said. "Oh y'all thirsty ain't y'all, calm down, y'all too hot in the pants." "Shit, we want a pretty boy too, you know we can't fuck with them lame ass dudes at school because they be on some other shit." "Right!" "I'll let y'all meet him one day, he cool as fuck, he goes to Henry Ford." "Oh okay that's a bet, I'm still talking cause low-key I would rather not get out this sexy ass car of yours Cash. Well before we go, can my girl get your number why she's acting all shy and shit?" "Damn bitch, why are you trying to put me on blast, I was going to ask him. Y'all just get out the car, I'll be down to your crib in a minute, Momo." "Oh okay I'll holler at you Cash, you're cool as fuck though my baby. She giggled. "Girl boom gone head now I'll be down there." "Thanks for the ride, playboy. They smiled.

Now we got some alone time finally, I should have made them bitches walk. She laughed, but nah they're crazy as fuck though huh." "Nah they cool as fuck though, real talk y'all seem like y'all have known each other forever, that's what's up you need some real chicks on your side, it's too many haters everywhere you feel me." "Yeah I do, most definitely they are some real bitches because they down as fuck, and they ready for whatever. If one fight we all fight ain't no one on their own this way. My bitches, we ride or die real talk." "Oh that's what's up, that's real shit because people be fake as fuck now a day. I know, you know, these chicks are a lot harder to deal with than guys are." "Yeah that's the truth if you ain't never told it before."

Cash said: "Well I got a couple of questions for you, how was your upbringing, how is your relationship with your mother, and when am I going to be able to take you out on the town my baby?"

In my head I think if the first two questions don't come out right, I'm uncertain if the last one is even an option real talk. I know if she's been abused coming up she's going to be a problem that I'm not in the mind state to deal with because I know how I came up, and it wasn't cool at all. So, I couldn't imagine my life in a girl's perspective, she will be all kinds of fucked up. I can't really deal with all that right now because I got a lot to be focused on. Plus, her mom had to be around because if not, she's going to have love issues of some sort, or she'll be a little on the wild side. So if she doesn't get along with her mom, she'll have a hard time dealing with authority coming from people of age, so that's a no-go. My family doesn't play the disrespect shit even my mom, although she had her problems; she still wasn't going to let no one disrespect her. My grandparents didn't play that either, they were quick to put a bar of soap in your mouth. Then tell you to drink some water and maybe that will cleanse your soul. That's some real shit they would do, I was eager to hear what she has to say, so I let her talk. Here comes the thriller in Manila!

"If you must know Cash, first off, I had a pretty good upbringing I was raised by my dad most of my life, my mom was around, but my dad had custody of us. I have two other siblings, an older sister who is 21 in a younger brother who's 12, I'll let you meet them someday here soon. My mom didn't make as much money as my father, so he won custody of us, but we just lived with him throughout the week and on the weekends, holidays, in the summer he let my mom keep us. I'm guessing you know why he was the life of the party of course, he couldn't stay out of the club, but he made sure home was taken care of first and foremost.

My dad is cool as hell he still thinks he's in his 20s of course when you meet him, he'll tell you he's 27, but we know that's a lie he's really 47, but he looks young. He keeps a clean shaved face, a pencil thin mustache, and he's always competing with my little brother Ricky with his waves. And every time they see each other they say, "you're wavy up top, but you ain't winning though. She laughed. They're both crazy as hell, my little brother funny as fuck too. He swears he's a comedian, wait until you meet him, he's going to try you with a joke off the top. My dad going to be talking about your waves to because I ain't gone lie it look like you got a 360 kit in your shit. Those waves are going ham I swear it look like a bee hive no exaggeration at all.

My older sister is cool as well she on her grown shit though she goes to Ohio State because of her boyfriend from East Cleveland. You know everybody was talking shit to because that's our biggest rival in the world. I intend to go to Michigan State, so we're going to have a little beef. She giggled. That's cool, I still love her though as always, she's my right-hand bottom bitch. As far as my mom we're the best of friends on some mother, daughter type shit, we tell each other everything. We hold nothing back, everything is straight up with us. If I'm having trouble with something I go straight to her first and if she has trouble she comes straight to me. We relate on numerous things, we have had our differences, but we nipped them in the bud and kept it moving.

My mom keeps it 1000 with me on some real shit, we don't lie to each other about anything at all, you would have thought we were sisters if you didn't know any better. I've really grown close to her because when I'm around some of my friends parents, they're beefing all the time and crazy shit like that. Then they get around my family and fall in love because of how close we are. It's spectacular to make them feel more at home when they're not at home.

My grandparents on both sides are really cool as hell, on my mom side you got the hip hop grandparents who listen to rap and has the nerve to be doing the Lean Wit It, Rock Wit It. She laughed, on my dad side they're more old school rhythm and blues, jazz, and soul music types of players. The rap doesn't get any play real talk, but they are cool, they talk shit and joke around. I got some cool aunts and uncles that be trying to school somebody every chance they get. We have family reunions every year on both sides in the summer, and they are live." Her phone lights up and dad comes across the screen. "This is my dad, Cash, hold that thought."

CHAPTER 15

THE THOUGHT

"Hello, what's up dad?" I could hear his voice through the phone, it was raspy like Lyfe Jennings. "What are you doing, I haven't heard from you since lunch when you text that oh crazy stuff about some girl that farted loud as hell and stunk up the whole room?" "I was dying when I read it, you know your ass crazy baby." My ear really tuned in then, was that her dad or her man like Sam said earlier. She didn't look surprised or shocked, so I kind of felt cool about it. Then she responded. "Dad, you're crazy, if you had heard it or smelled it, it was worse than one of your farts before you get a colon cleanse real talk. She laughed. I'm on the way home though, I just was talking to a friend; I'm safe though, no worries." "Oh okay baby I just was checking because I know you are usually home by now, your brother is here, so I know you don't be too far behind." "I got everything under control pops, I'm chilling, so I'll be home shortly." "How was your day in school, I'm hoping well I had a good day at work anyway though." "I had a good day, I'll be in the house shortly." "Oh keeping it short, you

must be with a boy huh, I'm starting to get hip to you now a day."
He laughed. "Bye dad, bye, bye you think you know me huh." She
giggled. "I will kick it with you soon, tell him I said what's up doe."
"I'm pretty sure he heard you himself." She laughed, "He said hey,
and dad I'll talk to you later!

My dad nosey, ain't he, I swear he thinks he knows everything."
"He sounds cool as fuck, if you were my daughter I would have been
like get your ass home out there being hot in the pants." I laughed.
"Nah you think that until you have kids of your own it changes
your mind, so they say from what I've heard. They were going to be
the strictest parents someone ever had, so you see how that turned
out, right." She laughed. "I know my parents are the coolest! Fuck, I
couldn't imagine if they were on some other shit, I would not know
how I would be." "Well, I'm glad you came up in a better way than
me because I was going to be like it's going to be hard dealing with
a girl who's been deprived of love. I know it's not easy going through
life without a father and a crack head for a mother.

To be honest, I didn't even know my mom for a long while.
People like my teacher and students used to talk shit about my
mom. I even talked shit about my mom because I didn't know it
was her they were talking about. The bad part is that I was living
with her and didn't know her name; I know it sounds crazy, but it's
true as fuck. I was also getting molested by my babysitter's and I
thought it was cool until I mentioned it to my mom, and she flipped
the fuck out, start crying and all.

I might be getting too deep, but I fuck with you, on some real
shit you've been keeping shit 100 with me all day, so I guess I feel
comfortable around you. Real talk I want to meet your people because they're way different from the way I grew up, I don't know
that part of family life."

"Yeah I'm a let you meet them one of these days, what else you got planned for today I'm about to go, I got some homework and cooking to do." "Oh okay that's what's up, oh you cook huh, I'm a need a meal one day if you know what I mean." "Yeah, I know, my pops always be talking about the way to a man's heart is through a man's stomach." "Yeah, you could say that is true because we have to eat you dig. Can you really cook, or you just be playing in the kitchen like some people I know because if you burn up the kitchen you're going to burn down the house? We both know that if the house burns down, ain't a thing getting cooked. I laughed, but I'm a let you go ahead because I got some homework to do plus you know I got practice at 4:30 p.m. anyway. I will be a little late, but you know I'm good." "Oh yeah, I'm a have to stay after to come watch you scrimmage one day since you balling." She laughed. "Yeah, come see me, why you don't cheerlead?" "Because I don't really like being with all them groupies and plus I did that in middle school, it's played out, if you know what I mean." "Yeah I feel you real talk they do be dick sucking extra hard when we don't pay they ass no attention."

"Yeah that ain't me as you can see, but my dad plays ball with his boys all the time. They be outside looking like the movie The Brothers with Morris Chestnut, D.L. Hughley, Bill Bellamy, and Shemar Moore. I be rolling watching them ball, so I know he's going to want to play you when he finds out you play." "Okay, I'm ready whenever he wants to get it." "Well here's my number boo don't act like a stranger, I don't mind talking, we should talk tonight if you don't mind." "Nah I don't, but that's cool with me, I don't have anything better to do tonight why not cake with you. Furthermore, before I go, Cash, can I taste them lips of yours?"

Before I could say a word I taste candy apple lip gloss, she grabbed my bottom lip with a vicious motion I was only imagining how she can suck a dick. Then I felt her hand rubbing on my six packs, her tongue in my mouth moving like the soft ocean water waves, she started to ease her way down my True Religion jeans. My belt was a little tight, so she found her way to get my belt loose. Our lips still locked tight: the moment is getting hot my dick is getting hard, I know her pussy has to be wet, the way she's making the moves on me. So, my only thought was to go down her pants; she only had on leggings, so it was easy. My windows are five percent, so no one could see in at all.

Once her hand was on my dick, I knew I was good to touch her pussy and if not, she had already let me fill it outside hurt leggings. She's stroking my dick at this point, so I had to feel her wet pussy. I slide my hand right in, she has some wet pussy, her thong in the front was soaking wet. I didn't even notice the front of her leggings with leaking pussy juice; it was crazy, like she already came before I got my hand in. It smelled just like strawberries, I swear to you, I have never wanted to eat a girl out right off the jump. Shit, as a matter of fact, if we ain't been dating for at least 2 months; it wasn't an idea that crossed my mind. I was about to cum, I couldn't hold it much longer. So, she pulled my dick out with my fingers deep in her pussy searching for her g-spot.

She was fucking my fingers so hard; I knew she wanted to fuck. She just didn't want me to consider her to be a hoe, but I knew she wasn't from the talk we just had, it was just a rare moment. She started moving, and I felt her about to cum, as she was coming, she put my whole dick in her mouth. Furthermore, she started sucking the fuck out of my dick, up and down her head bobbin like a bobble head, real talk. I came all in her mouth, but she kept going; she didn't stop. I'm shaking, I can't control it; I'm ready to eat her pussy and fuck her now, thinking what should I do?

CHAPTER 16

LOVE AT FIRST SIGHT

Basketball practice, homework, or pussy from the hottest woman in America right now, I don't need to think too long about that. Plus "Grind With Me" was playing in the background, but my coach going to be pissed because he doesn't play missing practice. He's been trying to call me, but I've been ignoring it, though. "Malieah let me taste yo pussy baby; I'm starving for it." "Are you sure you want to do that, you don't have to just because I did that to you, I just got caught in the moment." "Yes, I'm sure", I whispered in her ear, "Let's climb in the back seat." "Ok!" She climbed back there, and I followed right behind her. I pulled her panties and leggings down, then went down on her. Afterward, I asked her to ride my face. She put her knees-up by my head, and then she paused. She said I have to feel what I just tasted first. Furthermore, she sat reverse cowgirl style on my dick and start riding my duck. Clap, clap, clap, clap as fast as she could. "Daddy, this is your pussy ain't it; oh I love your dick, oh why does it feel so good? I love it all the way in me, keep grinding upwards, I love your stroke, daddy. Damn, this is the best dick I've had, do you like this pussy?" "Hell yeah girl, I can't lie I haven't had no one put it on me like this in my life."

Her pussy was warm as a hot tub and soft as cotton and the sight of her ass from behind was beautiful. The curves she had resembled a glass coke bottle. It was like I had a container of strawberries in my car from whatever she used to clean her pussy, I was going crazy just from the smell. She kept riding my dick something crazy, I could barely hold myself from cumin again because I felt her cumin, I couldn't help but let go. I told her that I wanted to eat her out, I was so ready. I needed it, I wanted it if it tastes like it smells; I'm a get it, and eat it up. She is bad as fuck and her pussy was just outstanding. I don't know if I'm going to be able to let her go, this is some of the best pussy earth offers. She pulled up off my dick, and it was juices everywhere. She wiped herself clean with a couple of baby wipes I had in my back seat. Then she put her pussy on my face, so I went to work, she started bouncing, then she started sucking my dick again, can you say 69 in the back seat?

I was falling in love on the first day I met this girl. What should I be thinking, she's mine now, or is this just a fluke because I'm lost in her body. She's all the way turned up; will I be able to tell anybody about today? This couldn't be true, am I really with her right now.

Then I snapped out of my daze it was all a daydream "What The Fuck", I was hard as a rock our lips locked, and she said, "I'll see you tomorrow Cash, have a safe ride to practice don't ball too hard my baby. Bye boo, call me later when you got time." "Oh, I will Malieah, for sure ; we got some talking to do, see you tomorrow." The car started up, she opened the door and smiled as she exited. Her girls were still outside sitting on their porch chilling, so she walked up to them and started talking. I pulled off as I saw them waving, I turned on some Gucci and headed to school.

I was pumped up and ready, I could feel a different energy. I showed up to basketball practice moving 100 miles per hour, making everybody play hard as fuck; they were looking at me like I was crazy. The coach was like, "Aye Cash you good, you playing like you just took some speed and got some pussy last night," he laughed. "Yeah, coach I'm good, I'm just hype that's all, I had a good day I'm ready for action. Somebody has to step it up so that we get the best practice we need." We played non-stop up and down the court until time was up, and then we hit the showers.

I got dressed, went to the crib, did my homework, ordered some pizza, and watched TV all while I thought about Malieah. So, I text her, "What up doe my baby, how are you living and what are you doing?" She replied, "Nothing, chilling, watching TV; oh this must be cash huh!" I replied, "Yeah, you know what it is." She said, "Call me at 9:30." I replied, "Okay, I got you." I dozed off and 10 o'clock hit, so she texted me again, "What you are doing, I miss your voice."

I jumped up and called her and on the first ring she picked up with a soft sexy ass voice saying, "Hello my baby, what you are doing. You must have fallen asleep, or were you busy?" "Yeah, I had fallen asleep for a second, real talk." "How was your practice and your homework?" "It was good; I was super hype after leaving your site. The coach was like you got some pussy last night or are you on some speed?" "Wow, he's crazy, I can't believe Coach K really said that, but he is down to earth as fuck. He cool, I can't imagine him mad, he's so happy-go-lucky." "Yeah, he is cool as fuck, we keep shit real. He likes for us to put our all in every time we come out to practice." "Did you get your homework done boy, I know you be playing. All y'all on the team slack off when y'all good and have skills." "Yeah I did my homework why you sneak dissing, ha ha ha, did you do yours while you are talking." "Yeah, I did my shit, it was long as fuck and kind of hard; I'm not that good at math." "Oh that's my favorite subject, I love math I guess I'm a have to get you up to par on math; it's easy once you start to understand how it works. I only have trouble in economics and history; I can't seem to grasp the concept of the two." "I'm shocked because I love those subjects. They are a lot easier than math; I don't know what you're talking about." "Oh well, we're going to have to work together on this school work because we both know what the other one has trouble in, isn't that a coincidence."

"Yeah that's crazy, I guess it was meant to be that we met because you're cool as hell real shit." "What's your favorite color, my baby?" "I love purple and pink, how about you? "Mine are red and turquoise; what do you do for entertainment?" "I like to go to the movies, out to eat, clubbing on the weekend, swimming, playing video games, bowling, going to the park, watch videos, doing hair, barbecuing, shopping when I get some money, and playing pool, how about you?" "Shit, you hit it all on the head, except I don't do hair and I like to hoop, play football, go to the beach, amusement parks, ride bikes, go to the gun range, shoot dice, play poker, and drive everywhere since I got my license." "Oh, that's a lot of stuff, what kind of bike you ride?" "I got a 750 Ninja; I'm pretty good on it, too." "OMG, I'm going to have to get on the back of that one day." "Yeah, yeah, I got you no problem." "What qualities do women you date usually have?" "Well, I like strong-minded, smart, sophisticated, high self-esteem, loyal, respectful, honest, pretty, nice, generous, well-mannered, creative, and many more. But that's some of the most important ones, how about you?" "Well, there's not many more than what you name Cash, all those and a good relationship with God. God is significant because he comes first." "Yes, Lord, say that again; he's the only reason I'm able to talk to you today. How long have you been single, if you don't mind me asking?" "Well, like seven months, these guys, just been on some other shit lately. My last boyfriend just did me wrong, he couldn't stop hitting on me or cheating. I was unable to deal with it no longer, so I broke it off with him. It's getting late as well; not that I don't want to talk, but I'm going to be sleeping in class." "Okay, we can talk more tomorrow; I can't wait to see you." "Me neither Cash, goodnight bye." "Bye, bye goodnight!"

CHAPTER 17

MEETING THE PARENTS

The next day, when I saw her after home room, she passed me a note and told me we should write notes back and forth from here on out. The notes got better and better as time passed, which led to us going out on a couple of dates, a couple of weeks down the line. We started kicking it really hard after that; we ended up going to the homecoming dance together, and everybody knew we were a couple at the time. Then she began coming to all my games to watch me perform; she even cheered on the side for me wearing my number on her shirt. Her dad even started coming to the games occasionally.

He and I got pretty cool, we would play ball all the time. He got the best of me left and right; he made me play hard as fuck. Furthermore, he was 6'3" and 250 pounds solid, no bullshit, plus he could ball for real; I had to play my heart out when he challenged me. I got better every time we played because I learned different ways to defend him. Before you know it, I was winning game after game. Then we started playing for money once he felt like I was getting the best of him. I think honestly he was just preparing me for the money I would eventually be making. I would play with everything I had in me for that money. It was 50 dollars a game; if I had 7 before he scored, it was double. So, I went for the kill every time, I barely ever got him to not score by the time I had 7. He knew I wasn't hurting for money, so he didn't mind challenging me to a game. As long as I was getting great practice, I didn't care who or what I played for.

Malieah and I had decided after 2 months of dating we would start having sex and opening up our relationship. I start picking her up for school and taking her home every day. If I had practice, she stayed with me, or I let her drive my car home if she wanted too. She had her license, so I knew she was okay, plus I let her drive all the time anyway, so she could bring me food after practice.

Then one day I met her mom and boy was she bad, man when I saw her I was like that ain't your mom. Her mom look like Kimora Lee Simmons with a banging ass body, she had a fat ass and some nice breast. She had in Asian accent that sounds sexy as fuck, I just wanted to hear her talk, and you better believe I listen to her every word. I talked to her for about an hour straight about almost any and everything. She's a straightforward and blunt person, but she kept it, grown woman. I fell in love with her because she didn't beat around the bush about shit; she already knew that we were grown in our minds. So, she asked us to just make sure we stay protected if we were going to be having sex because a baby is not hard to produce. She said I seemed like a pretty cool dude, I just better not put my hand on her like the last guy she was with because that shit ain't cool. I let her know I would never put my hands on her, but I would put my hands on another guy for her.

Two days after we had that talk, we had sex at my house. My mom was gone, and we had the house to ourselves. We were watching baby boy, and it got us desiring sex. She cuddled up on me and started grinding her ass on my dick, letting me know she was ready. Then she reached behind her body and grabbed my dick, I was already hard, so she caressed my dick in her hand. I reached in front of her, started rubbing on her nipples, and they became stiff and hard. She pushed my hand down to feel on her pussy, so I did. I rubbed on the outside of her jeans and started kissing on her neck. I flash back to when I was daydreaming in the car, then I got back to reality and put my hand down her pants. Yes, it was really wet and warm, it felt like warm Jell-O.

I played around in it for a while, then I had to smell it. Oh! The aroma of cherry came straight out as soon as I got my hands out of the pussy; I didn't even have to bring it to my face. I just start pulling her panties down I was so ready like Sponge Bob "I'm ready, I'm ready," except I wanted to get in that pussy. After I got her pants down, she motioned my dick in her pussy with her hands from behind. We started slow grinding from the side for about an hour and a half.

"Baby I love your pussy it has a hold on to my dick and doesn't let go, your pussy is great, I swear. I'm tired baby I don't have an ounce of energy, but I feel great, like I just won a championship game in the NBA. Hard play to the end, but the happiest feeling is to have won." "Daddy I'm tired too, to be honest, I haven't been worn out like that in a while, shit as a matter of fact ever. I'm going to be sore as fuck tomorrow, but it was all worth it, I love you daddy." "I love you too baby, this is really a great opportunity you allowed me to have, I must thank you." After that day sex was almost on the schedule everyday breakfast, lunch, dinner, and midnight if you know what I mean. We got along very well after that, if tension was up we released it quickly.

We started being around each other 24 /7 you couldn't get enough of seeing us together because there was more to come. It was the true definition of love at first sight which was going to last forever in our eyes. We loved every thing about each other, we understood we had flaws but we excepted them all. I was going through so many emotions of being loved by a woman in this way in my life I can't even begin to explain. I thought it was all about the physical aspects of a woman at first until she showed me the intimacy in a relationship. She showed me how to treat and love a woman through her love language which is completely different than the physical form. She explained every person has one of five love languages which are Act of Service, Physical Touch, Words of Affirmation, Quality Time, and, Receiving Gifts. We went on many dates to learn each and what we expect from each other sexually, spiritually, and mentally. Furthermore, we start preparing her for the ACT test to see where she was at for college. She could not wait to graduate because she was so over the high school environment. All her friends were glad she had someone who really looked out for her. They hated the last guy she was with because he used her and beat on her.

We got through her last year of high school fairly quick, when prom time came I was there, and it was on and popping. She wanted to wear pink and white, so we got everything pink and white. My tuxedo was all white with a pink shirt and tie made by Christian Louboutin, her dress was all pink by Christian Louboutin, shoes by Christian Louboutin and her accessories were Juicy Couture. We drove a pink Bentley Mousseline and had everybody going crazy because they have never seen a car worth that much in the hood. Then after the prom 3 weeks later she graduated and was getting ready for Michigan State. She left for college that summer because she wanted a head start on the game. We talked every day but spent the weekend with each other, so everything went smooth the whole time.

CHAPTER 18

COLLEGE

Now back to reality of my freshman year in college, man life is good, matter of fact life is great. I'm trying to see the big picture of what's all going on right now. There's too much attention coming my way, everywhere I turned bitches were trying to fuck me. I didn't know how to keep turning the offers down. I knew I had the coldest bitch out, but all the groupies were getting to me. Malieah was putting out enough to keep me satisfied, but temptation was always setting in. Every man has those thoughts of what another chick can give him. Super Head was trying to get me to sneak with her every five seconds. I had to bring Malieah everywhere I went because if I was out of her site I was going to get caught up.

I made Slam magazine front cover and at the photo shoot, there were so many models it was crazy, they were all over. Of course Malieah was there, she didn't notice that chicks went so crazy over me until that day. I also made GQ magazine because I was the best dressed player in college, on and off the court. My swag was crazy;

I couldn't help but be fresh to death. It's the way I came up, I had to be the center of attention because I was the Miracle Child.

When Christmas came around my freshman year, I decided I wanted to take a trip to Bora Bora resort because a couple of guys on the team told me it was super nice. So, I told Malieah to pack up some things that will last us two weeks, I was going to surprise her. She got all our things together then, as the day arrived, we boarded the private jet and were on our way. My thought was it's time to enter the mile high club, so that's what I did, it was a great feeling. We fucked for a delightful little minute in the air, aboard the jet, and we almost got caught. We had to say, "We're good, we don't need anything back here," because the flight attendant was on her way back to us. Finally, we landed, and she was still unaware of where we were, but when we stepped off, I said surprise.

There was a gigantic sign that said welcome to Bora Bora. Her eyes lit up, and she was smiling from ear to ear, she started jumping up and down. I had not seen her happy like this since my performance when I won the state championship. It had been a little while; only this time she was excited for herself. She told me that when she graduated from the 12th grade, she always dreamed of going to Bora Bora.

She didn't know I planned to get married over there as well; she had already picked out her dress because we talked about it. Furthermore, she just didn't know when I was going to pop the day off. I had set up for our parents, grandparents, and her siblings to be there the day before. So, they got everything ready and in place for the surprise on Christmas Eve, we were getting married on Christmas Day. As we got off the plane, our chauffeur took us to the beautiful hotel I picked out. We settled ourselves in, and I told her I have another surprise. "We are getting married." She said, "Huh." "We're getting married," I repeated. "OMG! Really, don't play with me like that, baby." "I'm not playing baby, everyone's waiting on us, so get ready; your dress is in the closet."

She walked over to the closet and tears of joy rolled down her face; she couldn't believe her eyes. She grabbed her dress and said, "Baby, I love you." "Now let's go, we have a time to meet. I'm getting ready now babe, your makeup artist is down in the back of the lobby. I'm about to call her up here." "Okay, I'm ready for her." "Alright babe, I'll see you down there, and I'll send your mom up here as well." I left the room to speak with our guest because I would rather not see her until the time was right.

They all were happy and excited for us; they couldn't believe it was all about to happen. She came out, and it was time to walk down the aisle, here it goes the lifetime commitment. We stood in front of the preacher and said everything he asked us to repeat. Here it goes the final words, "Do you Jason Jamar Cash take Malieah Diamond Smith to be your lawfully wedded wife?" I smiled and said, "I do, I do, I do oooh," everyone laughed. "And do you Malieah Diamond Smith take Jason Jamar Cash to be your lawfully wedded husband," she smiled and said, "I do." The preacher said, "You may now kiss the bride." We kissed for a whole minute straight. We saw pictures snapping, so we enjoyed the moment as much as we could.

Now that getting married was in the bag, it was time to enjoy our 2-week vacation on the island. We started by enjoying the nice water they had, it was crystal clear and the most beautiful water I've ever seen. Furthermore, we went sightseeing all over the place, I saw some remarkable art and beautiful people everywhere I turned. Not only that, but we went to some antique stores and seen so much stationery, novelties, and souvenirs that we wanted for collectors' items.

On our way back to the hotel, we chilled where they had a pool area. It had a water pool table in the center of the pool and a basketball rim at the edge of the pool. The hotel rooms were decked out to the maximum presidential style. They had full kitchens, full bathrooms, a hot tub, massage chair, mirrored ceiling, an awesome view of the beach, great room service, and anything else you can imagine. The activities they offered were kayaking, scuba diving, and snorkeling as far as the water sports. The available land sports were tennis, basketball, volleyball, and for entertainment they had pool tables, foosball, a casino, and a gym. They have a natural mystic massage or many romantic picnics for two. Also, available were private Jacuzzi style roman tubs that were decorated with rose petals and aromatherapy candles. They have big annual events like the Misses Bora Bora pageant and the Jerk festival, there's also the Mr. Bora Bora pageant in Boraween celebration. Most people go wild about their weekly theme parties such as Pimper's Paradise, where guests dressed in retro pimp or whore costumes. Their most popular one was Tease Me Tuesday, where everybody has to wear lingerie or pajamas. So many celebrities come through the beach, and that night g-unit whole squad was there just chilling and having fun. We partied almost every night, and we were enjoying all the activities they had to offer.

Before we knew it, it was time to go, time to get back to school and home. A couple of months went by, and it was time to be revealed at the March Madness games. Everybody had been waiting all year to find out who was pledging Sigma because we were the talk of the town and the most live crew at Texas A & M.

CHAPTER 19

FRATERNITY

We all came covered up, as in the ones that were getting revealed. Everybody was there; I mean people who had already graduated, moms, dads, grandparents, and everyone else you can imagine. We began stepping with our masks on and everybody was cheering and rooting for us, screaming, "Show them faces, show them faces." Once we finished stepping, we all lined up a foot away from each other in front the crowd. By that time I was happy as hell thinking, the day, and time has finally arrived time to become officially a brother from another mother.

So many thoughts began running through my head. I was seeing all types of different hallucinations from the thoughts I was having. I was the seventh in line of a group of 25 of us, so I knew my turn to reveal myself was going to be soon. They called for the first guy, who was my boy Marty. He stepped forward reached down to touch his toes, so they took our paddle and gave him one good ass smack. He took it like a G, pulled off his mask and faced the crowd. Everyone went crazy, all you could hear coming from the amped crowd was, "Marty, Marty, Marty, Marty." It was crazy after him my boy Chris went, then Drew, DeAngelo, Zane, Pablo, Zoman and finally, it was my turn.

Oh shit, I could feel the hit before it even came. My knees began to buckle, I felt weak and strong at the same damn time. Here it goes, the ass breaking hit everybody was cheering for the hit saying, "Tear his ass up, tear his ass up." They were so loud, I figured they wouldn't hear the little bitch come out once I get hit. Then POW, "Oooh, he'll yeah baby," I screamed turned around and through my mask into the crowd. The whole crowd went wild and began yelling, "Cash Money, Cash Money, Cash Money." I jumped up and down doing the boss up and get this money, "Shot out to Blade Icewood Detroit's All-Star Legend, R.I.P. Blade Icewood we love you Blade." Malieah somehow caught my mask and ran up to the front yelling, "I love you babe."

The next up was the other brothers which was Lil Len, Big B, Meech, Vinnie, Paris, TJ, Cork, Lamar, Bud, Ryan, Flex, Jay, Cheese, Twin, Tim, David, then finally Carl. We were finally a part of Q dogs, which is one of the greatest fraternities ever created. From there we stepped in tune back to the House of Sigma's. Later on that night, we had a crazy party after we showed back up to the dance. The after party had everybody there drunk and we had a good time.

Then came basketball again, and we made it to the final 4, but we got beat out by Florida State University. I got a chance to play in the All-American Game where I scored 48 points, 7 assists, 2 rebound and three steals. I put on a pretty nice show, it surprised plenty of people with that being my first appearance as an All American, and my team won.

After the year was over, it was back to summer camp and hard training for next year. I was looked at to get drafted my sophomore year, but I turned it down, I wanted a NCAA championship. So, I put my all in that summer along with my teammates, we were determined to win. I knew we all had it in us from last season, so we put our big loss behind us and played our best game.

The season came up faster than we thought, but we were ready our first ten games, we blew them out of the water by 15 plus. The next couple of games were really close, but we won by two or three, so we were undefeated. We jumped back up to winning by ten plus the next nine games. We almost lost the tenth game that went into double overtime, a close game which we won by one point, the final score was 103 to 102.

We watched that tape over and over again to figure out where we needed to improve. The reason being, that game should have not been so close, even though they're a great team. We saw all the missed shots, the lack of defense, and all the open shots they had.

In the next games, we didn't give anyone a chance. We kept an eight to fifteen point lead; we were never down at all during the game. The new's castors and commentators were going crazy, they put us in every one of their conversations. Every magazine relating to or containing a sports section wanted us on their covers. We were breaking records left and right, making highlights every time we turned around. We played a few more games that we won and as March Madness came about, we were undefeated. It's a lot like I was playing in the video game on PlayStation 3 where I could control whether this season would be undefeated or not. We were the number one team, so we played the number five team; we blew them out from the start. Then the next two teams we played came close to winning as it was really close to the end. We played the next game with all our heart because we didn't come this far to lose.

Finally the Final Four is here again, but this time we are way more pumped up for the win, and we are not going home this time around. We were playing Louisiana State University, and they have only lost 5 games this season, so they were just as hungry as we were. When the game started, they took a 10 to 2 lead and kept it for the whole first half. The coach came to us and let us know we didn't have to win if we didn't want to, he will be ok. If we didn't want it, LSU definitely did, they were playing their hearts out. If we wanted it, all we had to do was just get our heads in the game because they're not better than us. All it took was the determination and heart to go out there and get the win we were looking for.

So, once the second half started, everyone turned up their game play times 10. We took the lead after the first 5 minutes by 3. Thereafter, we went up by 10 all the way to the end of the game. Now we made it to the championship games, it was the greatest feeling. I was also going to go to the NBA this year rather we won or not, my mind has changed. I was going to the first pick in the first round, I could not turn that down. As the game started, my team vs. Michigan State, we took an early lead by 8. By halftime the game was tied, and we had slacked off a little and the coach let us know where we needed improvement. We used that to our advantage, the second half of the game we took the lead again by 10, and we weren't letting up. It was nothing they could do, the game was over, 104 to 92 was the final score, and we won, we won!!

CHAPTER 20

TEAM PLAYER

"What a hell of a performance, the Aggie's put on today and all year long. They have done the unthinkable, an undefeated record this whole year. They've played great from the beginning to the end. Furthermore, they were determined to win. Not only that, but they lost in a close game last year, and you can tell they didn't like that at all. No one seen this coming, but they've sure put everyone on the edge of their seats.

I've been watching them ever since JR Cash joined their team, they have been impressive. He's put the team on his back and carried them all the way home. He's the best thing I've ever seen in college basketball in all my years. Furthermore, he turned down the NBA last season to get a college championship under his belt. Besides, he's one amazing player when it comes to playing the game of basketball. I see something in this man who will have a spot in history. I really want to know what's going through his mind right now. He knows he's the first pick of the first round and his

Detroit Pistons have the first pick. He is going home, and they will be blessed to have such an astonishing player. The championship is his; he did what they said he couldn't and went where they said he wouldn't. Well, here he is, let's hear what he has to say about his performance."

"Hello Mr. Cash, what happened tonight? That was one great show you and the Aggie's put on. You scored 32 points, had 11 assists, 10 rebounds, and 8 steals, you came out to play tonight didn't you?" "Well, I did what I had to do to get my team a championship. I couldn't do it without the help of my teammates, and I'm genuinely thankful to have such wonderful teammates. They really give me the energy I don't believe I have in the locker room. They let me know that I'm the head of the team, and they're the body. So, with knowing that we all must work together to make a functional team that pulls through the toughest times. I'm learning so much about the game day by day. It's one hell of an experience to be playing on a championship team. We went this whole season without a loss, some were close, but we made it happen to get a win. The performance we put on was all team work; it wasn't just me, it took even our 12th man. Everyone chipped in to make the outcome end in our favor, I thank God first, then my awesome teammates.

I knew we had it in us to bring home the title, that's why I chose not to go to the NBA until next season. My teammates promise me that if I stayed with them, they were bringing home a championship. I stayed just to go for another chance at it because I knew I couldn't let them down. They wanted that title more than ever, and I knew a lot of them wouldn't be as lucky to go to the NBA like myself. I'm very humbled to be around such great players in the college basketball association.

I love the game more than anything I've ever been interested in my entire life, it's what I literally live, eat, sleep, and will die for."

"Oh ok, Cash, I hear you're the first round pick, how does that feel to be at the top?" "I'm still taking it all in, it's outstanding to be told you're the best player in college basketball. I used to dream of something like that happening. Being the number one draft pick just doesn't happen to just anyone, it takes a great player to even be nominated. I'm truly thankful to be not the second, third, or forth, but the number one is mind-blowing."

"What do you intend to accomplish once you get into the big leagues this season coming up?" "I'm not certain, I know it's about to be a different level of a ball game once I enter the NBA. They are more powerful and stronger players, plus they've been playing for years, so they have more wisdom. I'm ready to learn from some of the best that are playing in the league as of now and some of the best that's retired. I can't wait to show what I have to offer the game. Of course, I have so much to learn and so much to look forward to, but I know I'm going to have fun and do what I love to do until I can't do it anymore." "Who would you say are your top three influences that you've seen as an inspiration growing up?" Well, I would have to start with Michael Jordan himself.

As a young boy, I enjoyed watching his countless amazing performances. I used to try to imitate his every move and his style of play as an all-around player. Then you have Magic Johnson, who put on a show every time he came out, and he made a big name for himself. Then you have Kobe Bryant, who I'm not certain how he does it, but to see him play is crazy. He puts up shots something like Jordan and the way they fall in blows your mind, it's like a magic touch he has." "Do you think you will ever be one of the top players in the league?" "Now that's one of my dreams I can't even yet begin to say I'm going to be anywhere near the greatest, but I will try my hardest to get where I need to be. My only thoughts are to play the game and play it well so that I can get a ring one day. If I'm able to get a ring, then that's when I'll even start to say I'm anyone besides a college superstar.

I know it's some big shoes to fill to be labeled one of the top players the NBA has seen. I'm going to try to break a record of some sort, but I'm not sure what it will be or when. I also know there are some Hall of Famer's who have never received a ring, but that's not what I want for myself. Furthermore, I just want to say one last thing thank you, Lord, my mom, my grandparents, my wife, and my team I'm very lucky to have them on my side."

"That's all folks you've heard it straight from the horse's mouth, he's as ready as he can be for the future that is soon to come. His skills are official on and off the court in this here college setting, and we all seen his performance in high school. Now there is only one bigger thing that he could do and that's to get a ring with his Detroit Pistons. I believe that he'll do it, and all I can predict is massive things to come from him. He will definitely be remembered here at Texas A&M, and he's also going to be remembered at his high school Cody when he was a Comet."

There I was walking in the middle about to receive the MVP award along with the championship trophy. It was crazy champagne everywhere, people screaming and so much going on that you would get lost if you came with somebody that wanders off. We all started to go a little crazy, then after all the talking it was time to go back to the locker room. As we started to walk towards the locker room, all the fans were going crazy, I saw my mom and had a crazy flashback.

CHAPTER 21

FLASHBACK

Hard times came up because I was experiencing the happiest I've ever been. My mom had tears of joy rolling down her face, and it made me think about my tears of pain. Back when I was 5 until 13 years old, there would be days my heart was crushed when Christmastime and birthdays came around. I would be going to sleep hoping for gifts when I woke up from Santa, but it was nothing there. I would cry and cry in the inside and out, but nothing seems to help. Furthermore, I would ask my mom, "What have I done wrong that made Santa not come to our house and give me gifts." No matter how hard I tried, it would feel like Santa never came through. We had a little Charlie Brown tree that wasn't massive, but it was lit up. I used to just sit in front of the tree and wish that the gifts would just appear at any given time. My mom used to say that we are Jehovah Witnesses, and they don't celebrate Christmas.

I couldn't help but feel torn apart when school came back around because all the kids talked about what they got for Christmas. I would just sit by myself and try not to pay any kind of attention to any of them. I really hated show and tell time because I didn't have anything to say, so I'd usually just make some things up that sounded cool. Sometimes people would ask me questions about how I like it because they had this same thing and I would say I haven't opened it yet. I can't explain how tough it was to never receive any gifts, even though I was getting them all year long. My mom never gave me any of them, and at the time I didn't know I was even getting gifts from all over the world.

So I just was a sad kid who didn't feel loved and felt like no one cared about me. I was the lone lost soul trying to fit in somewhere in the world. I didn't see how people were happy, what was there to be happy about, and who was making everyone walk around with a smile. Not only that, but I was just the problem child in everybody's way, they had to deal with me because I was in their way. Day in and day out, I was seeking love; I walked around with my head down. I hardly ever smiled; I was built up of anger and aggression, while everyone else walked around smiling from ear to ear. The more I tried to look for out's and help, the more I got shut down. Life sucked, no matter how much people tried to cheer me up. It seemed like I got the bad end of every stick that was brought my way, life was breaking me off. There have been times when I would go days without smiling and days of feeling low down to the ground. I used to wonder what I was here for if no one even loved or cared about my existence. I even felt as though the kids I was around even treated me like shit.

I couldn't explain myself to know one because they never paid me any attention. Likewise, I felt as if I would have been kidnapped no one would ever come looking for me. Furthermore, I thought about running away to somewhere, but I had nowhere to run. Every time things seem to pick up a little, worse events came and stole my spotlight. I needed someone to turn to but, there was no one in sight, how was I going to last when my heartache of pain. I had no appetite for food to the point I couldn't eat, my mind was overpowering everything I did or didn't do.

I barely knew who my mother was because she was never there for me and when I did see her, she was high as a kite. People talked shit about her in front of me, and I didn't know who they were talking about. I even made horrible remarks about her not knowing who I was speaking about. Once I found out, I was devastated to know that's who they were talking about. I'm uncertain if some students knew, but I know for sure my teacher's knew. If the students did know, they must have really considered me to be a retard or a super lame. It really had me thinking that no one respected me if they knew but didn't tell me. All they did was subliminally make remarks about my mother and never told me anything. Even if they had told me what was going on, I still wouldn't have done anything to stop what was going on. Numerous people wouldn't have been able to deal with all the problems I deal with on a day-to-day basis. I know I'm one hell of a human being to have pulled through tragedy after tragedy and still be going. I can do anything in the world, I figure if I've already made it through all that I have. It takes a lot for a person to not give up, when that's the easiest way out. Not getting any love is what kills people every day, but for me, it made me stronger. They always say no pain, no gain, and I've been hurt so much that I can only win, win, win no matter what. I have money on my mind, and I'll never give up and when I step up into the building everybody hands go up; they stay there because all I do is win.

I was back to reality and there was music playing people yelling, jumping up and down. We got into the locker room and all the players were super happy. Our coach was crying and soaking wet from the Gatorade that was poured all over him. He called us to a huddle and said, "Guys, I knew you had it in you, it was always there, y'all just had to play as a team. Every one of you showed your presence in this game today and all season. I can't explain how you guys pulled it off, but y'all put everything you had in tonight's game. It's impressive to see a group of guys to do what you did this season. I don't think another team in history will ever put on a show like this. I'm genuinely thankful to have coached such great players. Furthermore, I've been part of true history here tonight, this will be remembered forever. You're all a real fantastic set of players and those of you who make it to the NBA I wish you well.

Now, Cash, you are one of the greatest college players to step on the court. Your talent and gift is out of this world; I've never seen someone do what you do. I'm amazed every time you come out of the locker room. As far as the rest of this team, you put your hearts into the game last year and made a promise and kept it. So, what can I say besides, congratulations, you guys got it done! I'm proud of you champions, yes I said champions!!!"

CHAPTER 22

CELEBRATION

Time to celebrate and party, party, party, I'm going all out tonight, drinks on me. We tore up the city that night it was crazy, half-dressed girls were everywhere. It was on and in full effect, so anything that happened, it was whatever. Malieah was right on my side supporting me all the way, I tell you I love her.

As off season approached it was time to chill out a little until the draft, so I went home to Florida. I didn't do much besides practice, spend time with my wife, and play video games. The draft came, and I was drafted to the Detroit Pistons, right where I wanted to be. I couldn't complain at all, I started summer camp with them, but I knew I was going to play no matter what.

They were looking for a point guard, and I was the best thing on the market at the time, standing 6'5" my rookie year. As the season started, I came off the bench in the beginning because they wanted me to build myself up. Halfway through the season, I was starting and playing 40 minutes a game. Going up against some of my inspirations was really crazy, especially when they would lecture me after the game. To let me know I have mad talent and I will go far if I stick to my guns. Playing ball was something that came natural to me, so I came out every time to play hard at what I love. My contract was for 50 million for 6 years, that's good money, plus I already had money before that.

My rookie year we ended up getting beat out the Eastern Conference Finals by the Boston Celtics. I still averaged 28 points, 7 rebounds, 10 assists, and 5 steals, which was pretty impressive for a rookie. I wasn't satisfied though, I wanted a ring, and we were so close to winning one I knew it was bound to happen. On our off season, I thought back to college and high school like if I did it then I could do it now. Everybody has been telling me that if I really put my all into my team, they would put their all into me. All I needed was a little dedication and hard work.

I trained along with my team like we trained in college; we did everything the same because this year we were getting a ring. I watched tape after tape to see where we got beat the worst at and what mistakes we made. We ran drill after drill, play after play, and training after training until we were one team, one fight. It was crazy chemistry brought out of every last one of us, no one ever knew we had that type of chemistry because it was just training, day in and day out. Everyone was in tune, not skipping a beat; we were ready for the season to start.

Our first preseason game we won by 15 points, the second, and the third by 20 points. Our first regular season game we had to play the Boston Celtics, we beat them by 19 points. We went on a 13- O run before we lost our first game, but we bounced back after that loss to 21 – 1. Subsequently, we lost two in a row, we had to tighten up even though we still had the best record. So, we went to 32-3 making headlines and being predicted to win the eastern conference finals. We lost again to the Boston Celtics by two, so we watched the tape and went in on the following teams, which put us at 49-4. I was ready for whatever came our way. The only teams that beat us were the Lakers, the Suns, the Heat, and the Celtics. We were ready to play all of them; I had seen all the flaws we had and all the flaws they had.

When the play-offs came around we were 76-6 the best record in the east. We played the New York Knicks first which ended 4-2 then it was time for the Boston Celtics, the team who'd given us trouble before. Our first game we won 103 to 98, our second game we won 113 to 90 and the third game we won 106 to 102, we knew it was over for them then. Their hearts were broken, they couldn't believe the upset that was about to happen. We were all the way turned up; we wanted a ring so bad that the last game they came out with their heads down.

The first quarter we took a 15 to 3 lead, and after they called a time-out, we went on another run 30 to 10. The second quarter we stretched the lead, it was 62-20 they couldn't pay for a basket, it was crazy. The third quarter it was 90 to 35, we were beating the hell out of them, so they just put their whole bench in. We put our bench in to play the fourth quarter and the final score was 110 to 50, we did it, Eastern Conference Champions. We were done and waiting on the Phoenix Suns and the LA Lakers to finish their 7 game series, which the Lakers won. So now we are ready for whatever; we would rather not take it to a 6 or 7 game series because Kobe Bryant pulls off incredible baskets in clutch times.

We won the first game by 8, the score was 108 to 100, but they won the second game 100 to 105. We were mad about that loss because it should not have even ended in a win for them because we were up the entire game. In the last two minutes, Kobe Bryant hit 6 three pointers back to back and no one could stop him. So in the fourth game we turned it up so that he was shut down the entire game, he couldn't get any points. The final score was 110 to 95 we put on one hell of a show, I scored 39 points myself. Then game 5, time to take home a championship ring we thought, but the Lakers came out to play. They beat us 89 to 111. We watched the tape, and they just out played us on every position.

We thought they were just playing with us before, until game 6 came around, and we buckled down and applied pressure to show them we have what it takes. By the second quarter we were in the lead by 8 playing our hearts out and not letting up. In the third quarter they tied it up, and we knew when the fourth quarter came they were better than us. So, we took another lead, that ended the quarter with us up by 6. The fourth quarter we intended to give our all to win this because if not, we are going home. We came out full speed, shutting down Kobe Bryant and putting points up. We made the lead 13 which it was only 5 minutes left. Then somehow Kobe Bryant got loose, he brought the lead down to 7 with 3 minutes left. Then the lead went down to 3 with 45 seconds left. We got the ball and tried to run out the clock but???

CHAPTER 23

CAN'T BELIEVE MY EYES

Oh my gosh, Kobe has stolen the ball with 5 seconds to go, but he's at the opposite side of the court. He takes two dribbles and throws the ball up in the air, it looks good from here. It falls short, it's an air ball, but it bounces up nips the backboard and goes in the basket. What a shot, it's going into overtime because he has done it again, that was unreal how did that happen. In the huddle up, I had to tell the guys what was on my mind. "I don't know how that just happened, but we can't let the Lakers beat us today, they don't have any energy left. We have to run and gun them the whole overtime minutes and shut Kobe down. When we go back out on the floor we need to use our full energy explosive nonstop, here all of you take this 5 hour energy. I need all y'all going nonstop, give them everything you have, and I mean everything. On 3 Bad Boys, 1,2,3 Bad Boys, let's go put some work in, so we can go home champions."

We came out ready, going strong and everything, I hit the first 12 points. We were up by 6, Kobe was trying his hardest to keep up, but we shut him down. This time around, we were up by 7 points with 2 minutes left; Kobe hit a 2 and then Hamilton hit a 2 right after. It was 50 seconds on the clock, and we were still up by seven, and we had the ball, they fouled me and I made 1of 2 shots and took the lead by 8 with 43 seconds left. Kobe came down the court and hit a three with 29 seconds left and took the lead to 5. He then stole the inbounds pass and shot a 2 pointer with 15 seconds left, making them only down by 3. I got the ball, they fouled me with 5 seconds left, and I hit one of the two which made it a four point game. They passed the ball in and threw it down the court but they missed.

We won; we are the world champions of the NBA. There was confetti flying everywhere, people were yelling and screaming. We did it we did it we finally did it we are the champions we are the champions, and we'll keep on fighting until the end. Will I be the MVP, or will Kobe Bryant be the MVP, he put on a wonderful performance this season? "The world champions Detroit Pistons have done it again; they have had an outstanding year, ending this season being 76 – 6. The MVP of 2007 will be, drum roll please, Jason cash is the most valuable player this season and his sophomore year in the NBA. He has taken a title home with him already, he has done it again. He has a Cody Comets High School trophy, an Aggie's Texas A&M trophy, and now a Detroit Pistons championship."

"Start with straight shots and then pop bottles pour it on a model shut up trick swallow," oh Lil Wayne has been playing and everyone was going hard, we were living out our dreams. The party was crazy; I thought it was something when we partied after my college championship, but this was a whole new tax bracket. I mean the money they threw just at the strip club alone was double what we spent; it was crazy how much fun we had.

After 3 days of straight partying; I went out and bought my first new phantom by Rolls-Royce thanks to Malieah blessing me off on it. I drove through the hood and everybody was geeked up and proud, we started a block party that very moment. Everybody I could think of came through to show some love, I had not seen some people in years. I paid for all the food & DJ and the activities for the kids, it was nice. We had all our local rappers come perform, and we even had some players off the team come by to show their presence. Everybody had a good ole time; they enjoyed all the music and games that were out to play. We even ordered the game bus to come through for us, and everybody took turns playing. Then as the night started coming to an end, we had fireworks to shoot off. After all of those things everybody started leaving, and I went in the house, the home of one of my boys I was staying in. I still had a room there that was untouched just for me when I came home.

Malieah and I slept until about 10 a.m., she got up to go visit her mom and I got up to check on the house. My boy was gone I was there by myself, so I decided to go clean up and plus I knew I had something I was supposed to be getting rid of. So, I went to the basement and started gathering some things I hadn't seen in a while. I have placed a lot of the things that I have wanted to get rid of on Craigslist. I had checked my email to see who all had sent me emails about the items, and I tried to call all of them. Most of them didn't answer, so I sent them voicemails emails and text messages to see who would respond. Then I looked at a box of games that I had collected over the years and I had a flashback.

I went into a daydream about my dad when I was little, the day he kidnapped me from my mom. I was just waking up about to brush my teeth while my mom was sleep. He came in and asked if I was ready to go to school, and I left with him. I thought my mom just had another one of her friends who usually just take me to school, so I didn't think anything of it. He went to my room, packed up my stuff while I brushed my teeth and we rode out. I didn't go to school, but my dad took me into kid heaven I thought because anything I wanted, I got it.

I got to go to sleep whenever I wanted, and I had more candy and sweets than you could ever imagine. I was eating steak, ribs, chicken, chicken tenders, hamburger, and lobster tail all week long like I was at Benihana every day. My dad would sit and talk to me then tell me my mom was going to coming to pick me up, but she never showed. I figured she gave me away, but I wasn't complaining because life was good, and I didn't have a worry in the world. I played video games all day long, eating candy and great food that was top of the line. Furthermore, I know that he didn't cook the food because I would always see a lady with an apron bringing the food. My room was so big it looked like my room at my mom house with our living room and kitchen all together.

Then my phone rang, and I popped back into reality and answer the phone, "Hello yes, how are you there I'm Larry I'm a game collector and I see you're selling your games." "Yes sir, I am, I have over 500 games, do you want to come check them out." "Yes, I'll be there in about 3 hours." "Okay, I'll see you when you get here." I took the games upstairs to sort through them, and then I saw a VHS titled "The closest to Death One Has Ever Been". I decided to pop it in for some odd reason or another, and I have seen the unbelievable, it was me on the screen, holy shit! Not only that, but I watched it for a brief moment, then all of a sudden, I fainted.

CHAPTER 24

THE CLEAN UP

Hey bro, let's get you to the hospital, I want to avoid waiting for the police and ambulance to come, they may take a long time. Is there anyone I can call to tell them what's going on before we leave out? "Yes, call my wife her name is Malieah, she should not be too far from here at her mother's house." "Okay, I'll call her!" The phone rang once. "Hello, hey babe what's going on, did you clean up our mess, and I'm on the way home in a little while." "Babe I need you to meet me at the hospital a.s.a.p I don't know what has happened, but I'm blind right now I can't see a thing and my eyes are wide open.

I was going through some of my old things in which I was going to get rid of, and I popped a VHS in my mom and dad made of me in the hospital when I was younger. I remember seeing what was going on, then I threw up until I blacked out after seeing my dad speaking to me." "Bay, Bay what are you talking about what video, how were you able to call me then, if you can't see and how are you going to get to the hospital if you can't see?" "Because I know your number and my phone by heart, anyway the man who came to pick up the games is here with me, he's who woke me up." "Huh babe, what's going on, stop joking around?" "I'm not, I'm serious, meet me at MLK hospital, we are headed up there now." "Okay, I'll be there in a few seconds."

"Hey Larry, I don't know what's going on, but thanks for the help, grab the movie and let's head out. My keys are in my jacket that's on the couch, can you please grab them for me?" "Yes, I got you brother, it's no problem at all, let's go." We got into the car and headed to the hospital once we got there and Larry escorted me into the hospital, straight into the emergency.

"I have this man here he can't see, but he said he could before he watched this video, his wife is on the way as well." "Sir, can you hear me, I'm going to guide you into the room, and my name is Miss Jackie? I'll be assisting you today as much as I can; I just need you to try to explain what has happened to you." "I'm known as the miracle child, I was kept alive right here in this hospital about 21 years ago. I was watching this video of my time I spent in the hospital when they were saving my life over and over again. I saw my dad saying die now, or you'll wish you had of died today, and at that point I blacked out; I don't remember anything after that. Larry found me dead on the floor, not breathing at all, and somehow I started breathing again, but I couldn't see a thing."

Now I wonder why me, why me, God what have I done to deserve this. I have already been through a lot, and now you take my site. I'm eating my father's words at this point, all I have is no good without my site; how can I enjoy any of it? Furthermore, I have lost everything but my life; I'm just ready to die. Not only that, but I hate life, every time something is going good; God comes and takes it all away. Likewise, I can't win for losing, can I? God must really hate me, I see; he just outright hates me. He tried to kill me as a child and if it weren't for the doctors I would have been dead; they worked hard on me to keep me alive. He allowed me to eat an eight-ball of crack at six months old. If he knows everything before it happens, why would he allow a six-month-old baby to die?"

"Cash, Cash, calm down! You're going to be okay, let them do a couple of tests on you before you say another word about God. You're just angry, mad and frustrated right now. Let them tell you that you are blind before you give up all hope because this might be a sign for you to get closer to God. He does not do evil at all; the devil will convince you that it is God's fault when things go bad.

Let me tell you about Job, who the devil came to God to ask if he could test Job to show him that he was only loyal to him because he had been given everything without working for it. He said you have always put up a wall of protection around him and his home and his property. You have made him prosper in everything he does. Look how rich he is! But reach out and take everything away he has, and he will surely curse you to your face!" "But see that's not me I wasn't always blessed with everything I almost died at 6 months' Job never experience that!" "Stop, let me finish the story, and maybe you'll understand me and more about Job. God told the devil it was okay to test him; take away everything but his health, so the devil did just that. He took away all his possessions: house, money, cattle, and children. However, what did Job do, tear his robe, shave his head bald, and fell to the ground to worship?" He said, "I came naked from my mother's womb and I will be naked when I leave. The Lord gave me what I had, and the Lord has taken it away. Praise the name of the Lord!"

So then the devil saw he didn't curse God, so he asked God to take his health and he will surely curse you to your face! The devil said skin for skin! A man will give up everything he has to save his life. So, God told him do as you please, but spare his life, so the

Devil struck Job with terrible boils from head to toe. Job scraped his skin with a piece of broken pottery as he sat among the ashes. His wife said to him, "Are you still trying to maintain your integrity? Curse God and die." Job replied, "You talk like a foolish woman. Should we accept only the good things from the hand of God, and never anything bad?" "So in all, Job said nothing wrong.

Now, do you see the faith he had Cash? The faith he had was true faith; don't let was going on physically cause you to curse God. He needs more faithful Christian children on his side because he only wants better for us, and that's the honest to God truth. Luke 15:1-7 Says tax collectors, and other notorious sinners came to listen to Jesus, the Pharisees, and the teachers of the law started grumbling this man welcome sinners and even eat with them! So, Jesus told them this parable. Suppose one of you have 100 sheep and loses one of them, what will you do? You will leave the other 99 sheep in the pasture and go looking for the one that got lost until you find it and when you find it. You are so happy that you put it on your shoulders and carry it back home. Then you call your friends and neighbors together and say to them rejoice with me, I have found my lost sheep. In the same way, I tell you there will be more joy in heaven over one sinner who repents than over 99 others who are righteous and do not need to repent.

So, Cash, have you offered your body to Christ or have you said God my first goal of my life is to know you better. To learn to love you and fulfill the purpose you have placed me on this earth for?" "No I haven't Mrs. Jackie, I do believe in God, I think. I just don't know what to think about God at this time." "Well Cash, receive Jesus as your personal Savior and Lord today, and you can go to heaven."

CHAPTER 25

COMING TO JESUS

"Baby, can you hear me I just got here; your eyes look fine, why can you not see me? What were you doing?" "Well, ma'am, we are going to do a few tests on his eyes to see what is going on." "Cash, can you see this light at all?" "No." "What about this light?" "No." "Look left and right. Well, your eyes are moving in the right direction. Look up and down and tell me what you see." "Everything is black, I don't see anything, it's all black." "Lean back, I'm going to put some eye drops in your eyes it may sting a little, but it will be ok. Then we will move your eyes manually to see what's going on, you will not be able to feel it because your eyes will be numb from these eye drops. Can you still not see anything presently Cash?" "No, I can't see a thing." "We looked behind your eyes, everything looks fine, there is no damage done. We will do an MRI on you to see if there's some damage somewhere we can't see with the naked eye."

"Malieah are you still here?" "Yes babe, I'm right here, take my hand." "What am I to do with no site? I can't enjoy life anymore, I can't see a thing, and all that I have really means nothing now. My hard work and effort to have the finer things in life is all taken away in the blink of an eye. You have to do everything on your own while babysitting a grown man. Do you intend to stay around if I can't see anything anymore?" "What are you talking about babe, why are you talking like that, that's crazy I will still love you, regardless of what happens to you. I'm not going anywhere, don't you ever say that again. Baby, your eyesight or anything else you have doesn't change who you are as a person, and it never will.

I have something vital to tell you, by the way, you are not going to believe it, but I'm pregnant babe. I took three different tests, and they all said yes. My mom was asking me what was different about me, and she told me that she thought I was pregnant. I don't know how she knew, but she did, and she had three tests over there at her house because I hear her and my dad are trying for another child. When I took the test, she was smiling from ear to ear, you know how her smile is pearly white and gigantic." "No way babe, stop playing with me; I know that you are trying to cheer me up, but don't play like that!" "I'm serious babe real talk, no lie I am pregnant!""Oh my gosh, this can't be happening right now I must be dreaming somebody wake me up." "Cash lay back down we still have another test to do on you then y'all can have some private time." "Okay hurry I'm not sure what's going on, but I need to be let in on this because none of this makes sense."

"We are all done now and I hate to be the bearer of bad news, but it appears that you have gone legally blind, is there anything else we can do for you? I'm going to set you an appointment to come back tomorrow, so we can look further into this. Mrs. Cash, just call us if you need anything before y'all leave."

"Okay, will do. Baby, what were you doing while I was gone?" "Nothing, while I was cleaning up, I placed a few items for sale on Craigslist. A couple of items sold, so I called the people, so they could come pick them up. Then I got in touch with Larry the gamer, so I was grabbing the games for him. When I noticed a VHS right on the table, I put it in and that's the last thing I saw." "I'm about to play the video to see what you last saw, babe, if that's okay with you?" "Yes, you're not going to believe what the hell I saw my dad say, I think that's what blacked me out." "I have it in."

Within a minute into the tape she says, "Babe that's you attached to all those wires, my gosh I know you told me about your hospital event I didn't know it was this bad." "Yes, baby, me neither until I saw it with my own eyes. I've heard stories from my mother and grandparents, but it's a lot more serious in person, I see why I'm the miracle baby. Watch my father's lips and tell me what he says, babe." "Oh did he really say that, let me rewind that again. Why would anyone say such a thing to their son, that's unheard of, I wonder did he really mean what he said?" "I don't know, but it blew my mind, I couldn't even believe it. I thought my dad loved me, but now I'm confused."

"Well, baby let's pray about all that's going on right now, it's a lot of answers that we need know and some that we may not get an answer. Lord, we come to you with many questions, while knowing you know all things before they happen. Things sometimes don't add up, and we find ourselves caught up between a rock and a hard place. We have praises and request for you in your holy name, you've blessed us with many good things in life. We sometimes go through very hard times which we know you allow brokenness to come into our lives, but the blessings that you have to come after the brokenness is why you are spectacular. Furthermore, we would like to know you better, and thank you in advance for all that is to come from your unconditional, abounding love. Oh! God, we are sinners, we are sorry, we repent, have mercy upon us and save us for Jesus's sake. Romans 3:10 says, "For whoever shall call upon the name of the Lord shall be saved." We know nothing is too small for you to be concerned about or too big for you to be able to handle. Matthew 7: 7-11 says, "Ask, and it shall be given to you, seek, and you shall find it, knock, and it shall be opened unto you, for everyone who asks receives. Everyone who seeks finds. And to everyone who knocks, the door will be open. You parents if your children ask for a loaf of bread, do you give them a stone instead? Or if they ask for fish, do you give them a snake? Of course not! So if you sinful people know how to give good gifts to your children, how much more will your heavenly Father give good gifts to those who asked him. Lord, we give you all the glory of our lives and keep us under your wings for all eternity. Amen."

"Well babe, I'm going to go see if you're ok to go home, and I'll let Larry grab the games from the house." "Hey Larry, can you hear me?" "Yeah, I'm right here outside the room, bud." "Okay, come here for a second." "Here I am." "Who's those games for, by the way, I seen you had said something about Jack would love these games for a gift on your message." "Oh, that's my son, he's right here with me!" "What you had someone with you, he must be as quiet as a mouse?" "Yeah, he's pretty quiet; son say hi to the man at least." "Hey Mr. Cash, I really hope you get better, I know you're having a hard time, I'll pray for you." "Oh Jack, hey pal, you know what, you can have all those games as long as you promise me you'll stay close as you can to God and listen to your parents." "I promise sir, thank you, thank you and thank you again, you're the best." "No, you're the best, Jack, and don't let anyone tell you different. You enjoy those games because I loved them all, but do your homework first because education is everything and the only thing to really be focused on."

CHAPTER 26

APPRECIATE YOUR LIFE

"Babe they said you're Ok to Go whenever we're ready they have nothing else to do to you. She gave me your appointment date and some sunglasses for you to wear, but I have a pair of Cartier in my purse." "Okay babe I'm ready, you see Jack he's the one the games are for, and I'm going to let him have them since he is so cool." "Oh babe, he's handsome as well, he looks like a good kid to be honest." "Thank you, ma'am, for the compliment." "He's too cute, babe." "Yeah, he sounds like a pretty smart kid." "Jack you stay away from bad people you hear me little guy." "Yes sir." "Let's get going, babe, grab a hold of my hand, I'll guide you to the car." "Larry, if you want to follow us back to the house, you can." "I'll be right behind you, I got the door for you."

"Thanks" "Babe, what's going on in your mind right now, I know you do not believe what's happening right now." "I don't know what to think right now, babe. Mrs. Jackie said some pretty powerful things to me, which let me know it could be worse. I actually want to take my life and give up everything, it's like I'm being punished for enjoying life. What makes me a factor in this world, if I can't see what I have? I feel like Samson, I might as well kill myself, I have no hope anymore." "What are you talking about, why would you say such a thing? Samson still was one of God's chosen, and he still served God all the way up until his death. He is still known for what good he did for God and His people; don't you give up on God now. I know your faith hasn't always been too strong, but now isn't the time to fall away from God who gives you the breath you breathe. You still have a lot to live for, just because your site is gone doesn't end your life. Many great people have come from being blind their whole life to being known as outstanding contributions of the world we live in. I know there's still so much to life you will have wanted to enjoy, but at least you're still right here with me.

Look at all you've accomplished at this point in your life, you just won an NBA championship with your dream team! There is a lot of work you can do to inspire others to live out their dreams, you have fans, Babe. People need you still; they still look up to you; I know if you put a ball in your hands, you still got it? I don't know what it's like to have my sight gone, but I know that your site doesn't make the very loving person you are. Don't worry about all the money and possessions you have because you can't serve two masters, you have to hate one and love the other. You will be devoted to one and despise the other babe; you can't serve God and money, you have to choose one.

1st Timothy 6:6-19 says, "Yet true godliness with contentment is itself great wealth. After all, we brought nothing with us when we came into this world, and we can't take anything out with us when we leave it. So if we have enough food and clothing, let us be content. But people who long to be rich fall into temptation and are trapped by many foolish and harmful desires that plunge them into ruin and destruction. For the love of money is the root of all kinds of evil. And some people craving money have wandered from the true faith and pieced themselves with many sorrows."

But you, Cash, are a man of God, so run from all the evil things. Pursue righteousness and a godly life along with faith, love, perseverance, and gentleness. Fight the good fight for the true faith. Hold on tightly to the eternal life to which God has called you, which you have confessed so well before many witnesses. And I charge you before God, who gives life to all and before Jesus Christ who gave a good testimony before Pontis Pilate, that you obey this command without wavering. Then no one can find fault with you from now until our Lord Jesus Christ comes again. At just the right time Christ will be revealed from *heaven* by the blessed and only Almighty God, the King of all Kings and Lord of all Lords. He alone can never die, and he lives in a light so brilliant that no human can approach him. No human eye has ever seen him, nor ever will. All honor and power to him forever! Teach those who are rich in this world not to be proud and not to trust in their money, which is unreliable. Their trust should be in God, who richly gives us all we need for our enjoyment. Tell them to use their money to do good. They should be rich in good works and generous to others in need, always being ready to share with others. By doing this, they will be storing up to their treasure as a good foundation for the future so that they may experience true life."

"How do you know that entire chapter, Babe?" "I study the Bible babe, I was taught to know the Word of God in my heart and my mind for protection by peace of God, and it's all through Jesus Christ. We never really talked too much about the Bible because I know we have some different backgrounds under our belts. We go to church on Sundays, but besides that, you never pick up your

Bible, and I always read mine." "Well, from now on, I want to read the Bible to me every day, so I can hide God's Word in my heart. I would like to go to heaven and I would rather not be like the rich man who dies then ask for pity; saying send Lazarus over here to dip the tips of his fingers into water and cool my tongue. I'm ready to give my life to Christ before I lose it altogether. Lord, forgive me for all my sins, I know I'm a sinner and I want to become just like you in all my ways." "Baby, I've never heard you speak like this, hallelujah." "I surrender myself Lord I would like to be free, I would like to be saved, take my hand, I wish to meet my king, and I no longer want to live in shame. I call on your name, lord, I was lost, but now I'm found." "Yes Lord, take him, my baby has confessed to you Lord; we need you more than ever.

We are home Babe, let's go inside and get those games for Jack, so they can go about their merry day. Sit down right here, babe. Jack, here you go they're all yours cutie." "Thanks Mr. & Mrs. Cash!" "You're more than welcome, you take care there Jack, please keep in mind our promise little bud." "I won't, you get better and get yourself some rest sir, talk to you later." "Cash thank you again; you're a real blessing brother. I really appreciate the good deed you've done, you couldn't have been a better person than you are now." "You're welcome and anytime you are in need, I'm here for you. Thanks for helping me out the way you did, you could have left me lying there helplessly, but you went out of your way to help. I can't explain how much that means to me, I could have never gotten up from my blackout if it weren't for you. You all have a blessed day and keep in touch" "I'll see you later."

CHAPTER 27

MY PURPOSE

"What would you like to eat, baby, I'll cook whatever you like or have a taste for?" "It doesn't matter, surprise me, babe." "Okay will do." "Can you call my mom for me, so I can tell her what's going on?" "Okay, where's your phone?" "Hello, hey son, how are you doing champ?" "I'm okay, but you're not going to believe what's going on." Currently, I'm at the house in Detroit; I just came from the hospital where I was diagnosed legally blind. "Do you remember the video of my hospital incident that you and my dad made of me?" "Yes, I'm not sure where that's at I haven't seen it in a long time, I actually forgot about that video. What are you talking about, you're blind?" "Well, I found the tape in my old junk that I was getting rid of, and I ran across it. I put it in the VCR and I saw it all; my father said die now or one day you will wish you had died today. I blacked out after I saw it, but this man named Larry came and rescued me by the grace of God. He took me to the hospital and Malieah came up there as well, and she watched the tape. They said my eyes look okay, but my vision is completely gone, I; can't see any light. I have an appointment on Monday for an MRI to see if it's something internal that they can't see. I have just been saved as well, I finally turned my life over to God and as of today, I can't live in the dark anymore. Malieah is pregnant as well, she just found out today she took three tests and all of them said yes." "Jason, hold on, this is too much all in one day.

Oh my gosh, my emotions are all over the place I'm happy, sad, excited, overwhelmed, joyful, glad, baffled, shocked, proud and more son. When are you coming home, so I can see you? And yes, I know what your father said in that room, and we got into a big argument that led to a fight for him saying that. He said it because he wanted nothing to do with me anymore, not because he hated you. He actually loved you; he wanted you all to himself, that's why he kidnapped you. That's my entire fault son I'm not going to lie about the situation, I made him say that honestly. He didn't mean any harm to you by what he said that day in the hospital."

"Mom, why me, why did so many things fall into place the wrong way towards me, it's like I'm cursed or something?" "No, son, everything has a reason, I promise you. Look at what you've been through as a blessing, now you're a follower of Christ. It takes different things for people to become a follower, and he wants every one of us to give our life up for him. You still have your life, it's not over yet, son; there's so much more to life than things you can see. I sometimes wish I didn't have to see a lot of what I've seen and gone through, but God works in mysterious ways. Everything will be okay son, just know you will have a much better life than this I can offer in heaven. If you come home by Sunday, they're doing a baptism next week, and you can be in attendance." "Yes, I will be there; I will be home by then. I'm just going to take it easy for the next few days. I'll talk to you later on, okay, love you mom." "I love you as well, God bless you bye, bye."

"Babe my mom said he didn't mean what he said to me, it was just that he didn't want to deal with her. I do believe that it was a lot going on between them, and he was probably tired of her at the time. After my appointment on Monday, we are headed home because my mom said they are doing a baptism at church. I'm ready to get baptized now! I'm feeling a hell of a lot better now; the devil has no more control over me.

You know, I used to have God as my right hand when I was younger. As things start looking up in life and I got older, I let him fall by the wayside. I let the money and the material possessions life offers take over my world. I stop feeling like I needed him because I had everything you could ever dream of. Who requires a God, I thought when I was my own God, I made my own rules, I didn't have to worry about anything and I did what I wanted. I didn't think about God because everything was given to me, or I worked for it by myself. I saw myself on top of life, someone who has been through all that I have and become a success. All my decisions were in my control, no one gave me the green light; I did all things on my own. When you get to the point in life when everything goes the way you want, you just totally forget God allows you to breathe. I didn't see the need for a higher power anymore; I wasn't struggling at all."

"Yes baby that's precisely what happened. You put your trust in your success, which is entirely wrong because God gives you everything you have. I'm about to feed you and then you can get some rest." "Okay thank you Babe I'll say the prayer this time, you always say it. Our Father who is in heaven, hollow be thy name. Thy kingdom come. Thy will be done on earth as it is in heaven. Give us this day our daily bread and forgive us our trespasses as we forgive those who trespass against us. And lead us not into temptation, but deliver us from evil. For you have the kingdom and the power and the glory forever and ever, amen." "Baby I'm proud of you it's spectacular how God works, now open your mouth. When you're done eating, we can get ready for bed, it's been a long day.

Monday came, we went to the doctor's appointment, and I was told yet again that my vision was completely gone. They did every test possible, it's nothing they could do to bring my vision back. It really made me realize that life isn't always fair or make sense. You have to believe in yourself and allow God to move the mountains set in front of you. Things don't always go the way you want them to but they work in mysterious ways for you to understand life for the value it holds. Just because you're given so many wonderful opportunities and options doesn't always mean that you won't have times where you're down or you won't take losses. Everything is a gift from God don't take that for granted you are blessed to be alive and able to do things the way you want. When one door closes another door opens always remember that. They referred me to a physical therapy doctor back in Miami to teach me how to cope with my illness and train me on how to get around. I also got a braille teacher to help me read books. I got home in time to get baptized that weekend as well. Furthermore, I started a foundation to help kids who have disabilities of all sorts.

I finally felt like I was put on this earth for a purpose. When you have all I have, you tend to forget what life is about. You look at those in need, only trying to satisfy your selfish needs. I know now how important life really is and where God's place in the world should be. People look at me for many things now that I've changed my life from thinking I had all control. I show and tell people to never give up because times get a little hard. You are what you allow yourself to be, don't let anyone or anything keep you from chasing your goals. Many things are hard to tell if you are doing what God would want you to do if you never go to him for guidance. I've seen so many beautiful things come out of the worst places or positions in life, I look at my life and say what a blessing it is to just be alive. Thank you God.